Learning intimate

D0824216

Sex, Love, &
Romance

Sex Education from the Bible

Crossroads College
G.H. Cachiaras Memorial Library
920 Mayowood Road SW, Rochester MN 55902
507-535-3331

By Hugh F. Pyle

Edited by Beka Horton

MINN BIBLE COLLEGE LIBRARY

MBC00000018962

A Beka Book
A MINISTRY OF
PENSACOLA CHRISTIAN COLLEGE
PENSACOLA, FLORIDA 32523-9160

Copyright © 1989 *A Beka Book* Publications
All rights reserved. Printed in U.S.A. 1995 C90

No part of this publication may be reproduced or transmitted in any form or by any means, electronic or mechanical, including photocopy, recording, or any information storage and retrieval system, without permission in writing from the publisher. Use of this material by or within any school in Escambia County or Santa Rosa County, Florida, is strictly prohibited without the express written consent of *A Beka Book* Publications.

Foreword

I have felt that a book was needed for youth between the ages of twelve and seventeen on sex education from the Bible. Therefore, I searched the Scriptures for all the verses on love, romance, sex, marriage, etc. that can be dealt with in a chaste and proper manner that each young person could use for his own primer on such matters. Questions are at the end of each section. The book is very practical; I hope it will inspire Bible reading on the part of each teen. In a class, two or three sections at a time can be covered, or with comment and question time a teacher can make each section fill an entire class period.

It has been my conviction that if a child is brought up on the Bible, and, if he consistently reads the Word of God as a young person, he will have all the sex education he needs. Why not let God teach our children about sex? Since the fear of the Lord is the beginning of wisdom, the warnings of Scripture about impurity and loose living will do much to prevent the sincere young person from playing with forbidden fruit.

The chapter headings give the thrust of the book.

Hugh F. Pyle, D.D., LL.D.

Preface
To Parents and Teachers

Young people need a certain amount of sex education. What many Christian parents object to is that often
such things are taught by humanistic, or immoral teachers who make no effort to teach from a Biblical perspec-
tive.

Many of us have been brought up to believe that
sexual matters are very private and that our children
should not have to be subjected to such mature information in their tender years.

Again, many parents are timid about explaining sex
to their children. Others want to do it but do not know
quite how to begin.

So why not let God teach our children about sex?
The Bible is the Word of God. I read the Bible through
when I was 9 years old, skipping many of the big words.
I did not understand all that I read, but this is where my
first sex information began. I do not ever remember
thinking that sex was a joke or a play toy when I was a
boy, though I had the usual curiosity and sometimes was
carried into fantasyland by my imagination, as most
children are.

I was sure that sex was for adults who were
married, and I learned from the Bible that those who

indulged outside of marriage, or who committed adultery, were guilty of terrible sin. Thus the fear of God was put into me, and "the fear of the Lord is the beginning of wisdom" (Ps. 111:10).

Does it not make sense that the best place to learn a thing is from the maker or the creator of it? "The entrance of thy words giveth light; it giveth understanding unto the simple" (Ps. 119:130). So, we can let the young people know how much we love, respect, and revere the Bible. If, indeed, they know that this is the Book to live by, they will approach its teachings and precepts with interest, reverence, and perception.

As a boy I read a few words in the Bible that I knew would be best not to repeat. But I also knew that I should not take what I read lightly. To me it was a sacred Book, and we were not to tamper with it.

God wrote the Book for young and old alike. He uses chaste terminology. He discusses almost every intimate thing the mind of man can imagine, but He does so to warn us of sin—never to entice us into sin.

We can urge the young person to have a dictionary handy when reading the Bible; also a good Bible dictionary is helpful. I did not have to ask my parents or anyone else about many of the things that puzzled me as I read the Bible, for I would look it up in the dictionary. That's where I first learned what "pregnant" meant. In the dictionary the child will readily and privately learn what such words as "travail," "buttocks," "ravished," "virgin," "womb," "circumcision," "concubine," "sodomy," and "bosom" means without embarrassment and without getting a dirty, sensual, or humanistic slant on the words.

At nine years of age there were many things in the Bible relating to human sexuality that I was not interested in or that I did not understand. At that age I did not need to understand it! But any intelligent child of 13, 14, or 15 can comprehend and get a good basic knowledge of these things if he reads his Bible and concentrates on what he is reading. It doesn't take long for a 12 or 13 year old to figure out what God is talking about when He says, "and Cain knew his wife," or "He went in unto her," or "who would have said unto Abraham that Sarah should have given children suck? for I have born him a son in his old age. And the child grew, and was weaned."

As they read this book on sex education, it will help them grasp what God says about sex in the Bible. Why not let them read it for themselves?

Remember, young people are absorbing a lot of misinformation these days from many sources. Teens, as well as adults, talk about sex freely and children often hear them. Many children and teens get ideas from TV, even if parents are selective in what is watched. Many young children talk about sex even though they don't understand it. Most of them have heard about herpes and AIDS.

Almost all teens know what you're talking about when you mention homosexuals or the (so called) "gays." A few years ago most adults did not know what a "lesbian" was. Now teens use the word as freely as they talk about ice cream or sports cars.

We should not give in to sin nor compromise our convictions. But we do have to take a different approach to the matter of communication with our children. Television has brought the world with its glitter and sin right into homes and thus into their young and tender hearts. Tots talk about things teens were ignorant of a few years ago.

Certainly we do not use the same crude words and filthy expressions the pagan world uses. But in chaste and careful terminology we can help explain God's own words on the subject. If we do, I believe we'll have a properly educated generation of Christian boys and girls who will reverence the Bible and will think twice before tossing sexual expressions about carelessly.

Certainly there are some things we cannot fully understand ourselves, much less know how to explain fully to the children. I refer to the multiple wives in the Old Testament, the seeming permission to have concubines, etc. But if we keep in mind that the Bible gives us a progressive history of God's dealings with His people and remember that they did not have the New Testament and the full revelation of truth from the Holy Spirit that we have now, it is easier to explain.

Some, I'm sure, wonder why God would even mention such things as sex with animals in Leviticus 18:23. This is filthy and revolting. But when we observe that it is discussed along with homosexuality in verse 22 we see how progressively debasing sin becomes. God wants us to learn that the human heart is depraved and desperately wicked (See Jer. 17:9; Isa. 64:6). And God faithfully warns us about such.

There are those in the twentieth century who wallow in such filth and indulge in Satanic orgies. Our kind Creator wants us to know that those who traffic with the Devil may fall to any fearful depth of iniquity!

God never leaves us wondering what the outcome of such will be. Leviticus 18:24, 25 tells us that if people so defile themselves they will be cast out as a people and that the very land itself will vomit out its inhabitants! God calls such base and repugnant immorality an "abomination."

So God is faithful to tell us the truth and to give us moral direction. His Bible is a book of warning as well as instruction. This present generation of young people desperately needs such warnings! And it is the purpose of this book to help the young teens have a moral conscience about what God says is right and wrong in moral values.

CONTENTS

Foreword iii
Preface v

The Beginning of Sex 1

    1 Sex from God's Point of View 1
    2 How Sex Got Started 3
    3 God Is Not Against Sex 5
    4 All Those Begats 10
    5 Two-By-Two—
       Learning from the Animals 12
    6 Good Looks and "Sex Appeal" 15
    7 Finding the Right Girl 18
    8 Boys and Girls Are Different 22

Love and Sex 26

    9 The Story of Birth 26
  10 Naming the Baby 29
  11 Good Grief! 31
  12 Love and Sex Are Not the Same 33
  13 Sexual Temptation—How to Handle It! 36

ix

Sex and the Scarlet Sin 40

14 The Scarlet Sin 40

15 Sexually Transmitted Diseases 43

16 Dancing and Sex 48

17 The Nakedness Question 53

18 Sex for Money 58

19 Dirty Pictures 60

When Giants Fall 64

20 Don't Marry a Pagan! 64

21 Many Wives and Concubines 67

22 The Playboy with a Hole in His Head 70

23 Samson—Sin Slays the Strong Man 73

24 King David and Bathsheba 78

25 Doing Your Own Thing 82

Romance and Sexual Temptation 85

26 The Romance of Ruth 85

27 So Help Me, Hannah 90

28 Fornication—the Boys
    Who Made Themselves Vile 93

29 David and "Dear Abby" 97

No Human Father 101

30 The Virgin Birth 101

More Bitter Than Death 104

31 Old Testament Soap Operas 104
32 Painted Faces 109
33 The Unborn Child Is Alive! 112
34 Our Secret Sins 117
35 Playing the Fool 120
36 Her Steps Take Hold on Hell 124
37 Like an Ox to the Slaughter 129

Sex Affects Body, Mind, and Heart 132

38 Health and Happiness 132
39 Where to Keep Your Heart 135
40 The Eyes Have It! 138
41 Sex and Television 142
42 Alcohol and Sex 147
43 Sex and Idolatry 151
44 Evolution, Sex, and Atheism 154

Young People and the Intimate Life 157

45 Who Owns Your Body? 157
46 The Bare Truth about Modesty 161
47 Learn to Say "Nay!" 163
48 How to Stay in Control 166
49 What Are You Thinking About? 170
50 Peer Pressure in Reverse 173

The Bride and the Bridegroom 176

51 Worse Than Staying Single 176

52 Not What He Bargained For 181

53 The Woman Who Is Priceless! 183

54 Learning to Love 188

55 Enjoy Your Marriage 191

56 "How Shall I Love Thee?" 195

57 Maintaining a Happy Home 199

58 Adultery and Divorce 201

59 Consequences of an Affair 204

60 Jealousy—the Death of Romance 208

Sex, Purity, and
the Judgment of God 210

61 Stay Sound to Stay Safe 210

62 Should the Priest Get Married? 214

63 Eunuchs in the Bible 217

64 Spiritual Adultery 219

65 Filthy Dreamers 222

66 The Final Judgment
     of the Sexually Impure 225

THE BEGINNING OF SEX

1. Sex from God's Point of View

We hear about sex on every hand. What does it all mean? It is most important to find what our wonderful Creator says about it. Sex from God's viewpoint is the best sex education to be found, for "It is he that hath made us" (Ps. 100). We are "curiously wrought," David said, and "fearfully and wonderfully made."

Since God wrote the Bible for young and old, by carefully reading the Bible, you will have all the sex education you need until you march down the aisle at your own wedding!

This book is not a how-to manual like so many sex-education books, nor is it a book on human anatomy. It is not written as a guide for adults who are married; more complete books and medical guides are available from physicians or pastors. This book is for teens who are beginning to form their moral values and who need to know what is right and what is wrong in

1

the area of sexual relationships and what the consequences of their actions will be.

What does God say about kissing, embracing, courtship, engagement, marriage, conception, childbirth, home problems, and divorce? Why not find out from the God who made us all? One young man wrote on the flyleaf of his Bible, "Inquire within about everything!" Just about everything that a single youth needs to know about love, courtship, sex, marriage, and child rearing is found in the Bible.

God told Adam and Eve to be fruitful and multiply. They could not do this without the sex act. Jacob referred to his family as "the children which God hath graciously given thy servant." God is in favor of love, marriage, childbirth, and happy homes.

The love of a bride and bridegroom is a beautiful picture of the Lord Jesus and His church (Eph. 5:22–33). Love is of God, for "God is love" (1 John 4:8). What the world so often refers to as love is nothing but animal lust, the fulfilling of a biological urge.

For this reason the love scenes in The Song of Solomon may be considered sensual and poetic fiction to the unbeliever, while the believer views the sacred intimacy of happy married love between two devoted hearts and sees the beautiful love which Christ has for His bride, the church.

2. How Sex Got Started

"In the beginning God" (Gen. 1:1). This is the best place to begin—with God. If we begin and end with Him, everything else will fall into place. Leave God out of it, and everything becomes a mystery, a muddle and a mess. "The fear of the Lord is the beginning of wisdom" (Ps. 111:10). That is the key. "The fool hath said in his heart, There is no God" (Ps. 14:1). You may be sure that what God says in His book is the accurate explanation for where we came from and where we are going, for "all Scripture is given by inspiration of God" (2 Tim. 3:16).

God told the original man and woman to "be fruitful and multiply." In other words, He told them to have children. It didn't take them long to figure out how to accomplish this. No "how-to course" was necessary, because God created them to know what to do when the right time came.

God made the first man, Adam, from the dust of the ground. Eve got here by creation from a bone—the rib the Creator took from the side of Adam. She was the "help meet," meaning a help suitable or fit for Adam.

Adam was made from the dirt and Eve from a rib. Where did the rest of us come from? How about the first two boys ever to be born? Genesis 4:1 says that "Adam knew Eve his wife; and she conceived, and bare Cain, and said, I have gotten a man from the Lord." God made Adam and Eve directly—by divine creation. Then He told them to "be fruitful and multiply," which they proceeded to do when "Adam knew Eve his wife." *To multiply* means they were to have children. This is where human sex began. God always uses correct words; He is never vulgar in His phraseology. So "Adam knew his wife," and nine months later Cain, their first son was born.

Adam "knew his wife" in the warm, intimate embrace of married love. God had married Adam and Eve. In God's eyes they became "one flesh." Such a sexual embrace is always for married people who belong to one another. Sex without marriage was always wrong in the Bible, and it still is.

Questions

1. *What kind of a person says "there is no God"?*

2. *What did God mean by "Be fruitful and multiply"?*

3. *What was the difference between the creation of Adam and that of Eve?*

3. God Is Not Against Sex

Sex is holy and beautiful because God invented it. God wrote everything that we need to know about it, and, regarding the details of married love, you can wait until later to find out about that. The Word of God has much to say about sex and gives the finest sex education in the world.

"Male and female created he them" (Gen. 1:27). In the arrangement of God it takes two people—male and female—for a new life to be produced. They come together in the intimacy of marriage, just as the Creator planned it, and the result is a precious little new boy or girl in the home. This is what it means when "Adam knew his wife."

In this intimate embrace of marriage, Eve "conceived" from the seed given her by Adam, and later Cain was born. The same thing happened again and the second child, Abel, was born. All through the Bible this is what is meant by "she conceived."

So sex is good, as God intended it, for married couples who have become man and wife. It is the abuse, the misuse, and the corruption of sex that becomes a dirty, sordid, and vulgar thing.

Today the world is at enmity against God,

and so sex is made a big joke and laughed at by the world. Unsaved worldlings sneer at what God says about the sanctity of married love. In the perfect garden of Eden we find that Adam and Eve "were both naked, the man and his wife, and were not ashamed" (Gen. 2:25). They were male and female—the handiwork of God. God made the intimate sex life a very pleasant and desirable thing so that His world could be populated with people who would love and serve Him. We are made "by Him and for Him" (Col. 1:16). God planned for sex to have pleasure associated with it so the human race would not become extinct and to assure that the earth would be populated with people. God made food to taste good and be appealing to the human race that man would have a desire to eat and by eating, man would be healthy and live longer. We know that people who do not have an appetite for food do not want to eat. Loss of appetite is a danger signal to their physical health. As the appetite for food is good for mankind—a blessing that God gave—so sex desires are also natural and God-given, but when sex desires are fulfilled outside of marriage it becomes a curse to a person.

God gave man a natural attraction for a woman, and He gave to woman an attraction to a man. So courtship has been around for a long, long time.

When Abraham and Sarah were old "and well stricken in age (Gen. 18:11), and it ceased to be with Sarah after the manner of women" (she could no longer bear children), God told them they would have a son. "Therefore Sarah laughed within herself, saying, After I am waxed old shall I have pleasure, my lord being old also?" (Gen. 18:12). There is real "pleasure" in the love life of a married couple. God made this delightful experience a thing of real joy for the husband and wife. The sad thing is that sinful men and women have decided they will violate God's law and enter into the sacred intimacy of sexual indulgence without being married. Thus, there have been many hardships and heartaches as a result. Illegitimate children have been born. Lives have been wrecked. Homes have been destroyed. Hearts have been broken. Abortion has been devised to kill little unwanted babies before they ever see the light of day.

This is why God thundered in the Ten Commandments, "Thou shalt not commit adultery." This is why God constantly warns Christians, "But fornication [sex before marriage], and all uncleanness, . . . let it not be once named among you" (Eph. 5:3). Not even *once* are we to veer off into this sin. So it is always best to stay out of the kind of situations that would tempt one to illicit (wrong) sex.

Young people often think that married adults don't have any fun, that they are pious, dignified antiques who could not possibly understand the whims, desires, and feelings of single teens. Don't kid yourself! Married people in love have a wonderful time. In Genesis 26:8 a Philistine king had thought that Rebekah, the wife of Isaac, was really his sister. But one day the king looked out a window "and saw . . . Isaac was sporting with Rebekah his wife." Isaac was pampering, petting—probably kissing his wife. To this Philistine king that was great "sport." It is, indeed, a very sporting thing. Husbands and wives who love each other do have a wonderful "sporting" time, I assure you. Usually we find it proper and discreet to do such lovemaking indoors with the shades drawn.

Young people who wait until God gives them their very own mates for such "sporting" love will save themselves a lot of grief.

Questions

1. What was the main purpose of sexual union between husband and wife?

2. Why was the fact that Sarah "conceived" so amazing?

3. What are some of the sad results of intimacy before marriage?

4. Necking, petting, or smooching were called what in the book of Genesis?

4. All Those Begats

When the first children on earth were born, Genesis 4 simply states that Eve "conceived, and bare Cain, and said, I have gotten a man from the Lord. And she again bare his brother Abel." People lived to be hundreds of years old in those days. Adam and Eve had many, many other children later, besides Cain and Abel. That's how Cain got his wife, by the way. God had to permit marrying within the family, at first, in order to get the human race going.

After Adam's immediate family, we find that instead of saying, "he went in" or "she bare a son," the Bible usually just shortens the sentence and says "she bare" or often, "he begat." To beget meant to *sire* or *father*. "And Seth lived after he begat Enos eight hundred and seven years, and **begat** sons and daughters" (Gen. 5:7).

"And Noah **begat** three sons, Shem, Ham, and Japheth," (Gen. 6:10). "And Cush **begat** Nimrod" (Gen. 10:8). They were together as man and wife, thus they bore or "begat" children.

Married people are to have children, not abort or destroy them. "Lo, children are an heritage of the Lord: and the fruit of the womb is his reward" (Ps. 127:3).

God encourages the husband and wife to

become the father and mother of children (Ps. 128). It is God's plan for the ideal home. The parents are to fear and love the Lord; they are to labor to accumulate the things they have and are happy in so doing. The wife is like a "fruitful vine" as she brings the little ones into the home. It is shown here that God delights to see the children about the tables in the family circle. The Lord looks down and blesses such a home. Another joy is shown where the grandchildren bring great joy.

So families, where possible, are to "beget" children. The Bible does not say how many or how few, but certainly we are never to abort them.

Questions

1. *The Bible usually said "bore" when talking about the mother giving birth. What does the word "begat" mean?*

2. *How is the wife to be a "fruitful vine"?*

3. *What chapter in the Bible encourages a husband and wife to have children?*

Two-by-Two—
5. Learning from the Animals

When God told Noah which animals to bring into the ark, we observe that He made it plain that He wanted two of each kind "to keep them alive"— that is, to preserve those animals. God said, "they shall be male and female." Isn't it interesting that the animals needed no sex education course? God built into them the desire and the know-how of reproduction in each animal—male and female.

Most kids who are brought up on a farm, or around animals, quickly catch on that it is the uniting of the male animal with the female that brings about the litter, the brood, or the calf, as the case may be. I read my Bible when I was a boy, but I also had a pet dog, and furthermore, we usually had a cow when we lived far enough out to make that possible. Sometimes I'd have to help my Dad as he escorted the cow over to some farm where she could meet her bull-headed friend— "husband!" Later a calf would be born.

This was part of my sex education. Reading the Bible was most of it. My Dad also reminded me that when people began "fooling around" before they were married, it always meant heartache and trouble. My parents taught me (and my pastor did, too) that husbands and wives were to be true to their own partners. Anything else was awful, terrible adultery. They were right!

In Gen. 30 Jacob proved that he had learned a lot about animals and how to get them interested in their own kind for the purpose of keeping the strain alive. Some of what he did is still a mystery.

In Job 21 God tells us that successful people have bulls that gender and fail not, and that "their cow calveth, and casteth not her calf" (Job 21:10). So God teaches us about sex and reproduction throughout His wonderful Word. We can learn from the animals.

In Gen. 1, God made them male and female. God said to the animals and fowls He had made, "Be fruitful and multiply and fill the waters in the seas, and let fowl multiply in the earth." The living creatures such as cattle, creeping things and beasts were to bring forth others, always "after their kind."

Soon after God made man and woman, He put them in the garden with the instruction to "be fruitful and multiply." If Adam and Eve had any doubt at all about how reproduction was to come to pass, remember they already had the animals (for examples) bringing forth. They needed no other sex education!

Questions

1. *Why did God make sure Noah brought into the ark the animals "two by two"?*

2. *Why do animals need no courses on sex education?*

3. *What are people who become "sexually active" without being married acting like?*

6. Good Looks and "Sex Appeal"

There is nothing wrong with wanting to look your best. Christian young people should not be slovenly and sloppy looking in their appearance. If we are to let our lights shine before men (Matt. 5:16), then we ought to look our best as well as *be* our best for Jesus.

In the Bible God mentions that Rebekah was "very fair to look upon" (Gen. 24:16). Abraham was afraid other men might be attracted to his wife, Sarah, for she was "a fair woman to look upon" (Gen. 12:11). Ruth the Moabitess was so striking that the wealthy and eligible Boaz fell for her at once (Ruth 2). There is reason to believe that Joseph was a very handsome young man (Gen. 39), that men like David and Samson had a great appeal to the women of the day. God is the one who made these people and others attractive.

However, the Bible warns us about letting ourselves be attracted to those of the opposite sex solely on the basis of their physical appeal. The fair Jewish maiden, Esther, was so beautiful that the King Ahasuerus was overwhelmed by her beauty. Yet Esther was a lovely and devoted young maiden who did nothing to try to lure the king. He just "fell" for her and soon insisted that she was the one to become his queen. The modest women of the Bible did nothing to arouse men by the way they dressed, looked, or walked.

We know that some people are just more appealing than others. God has purposely given a certain amount of appeal (sex appeal and otherwise) to bring about the courtship, the marriage, and the reproduction that He wanted for our good and for His glory.

Sarah was so beautiful that even in her old age a pagan king fell for her and would have taken her unto himself, if God had not stopped him (Gen. 20).

The "strange woman" Solomon wrote about had lips that did "drop as an honeycomb" and "her mouth is smoother than oil" (Prov. 5:3). She evidently painted herself in such a way and talked in such a sexy manner as to lead men astray so that "her end (the end of the party or affair) is bitter as wormwood, sharp as a twoedged sword." Solomon goes on to say that "her feet go down to death; her steps take hold on hell." This woman had sex appeal of the wrong kind.

God warns young men about the flattery of the tongue of a "strange woman" (Prov. 6:24). He commands young men not to lust after her beauty in their hearts nor let her "take him" with her beckoning (winking) eyes.

So there is such a thing as sex appeal, and young men need to be aware of it and not be taken in by it. Girls, too, need to be careful to admire a boy because of his character, strength, and integrity, and not just because he is physically attractive.

Television and the other colorful lures of the world constantly bombard us with things that are fleshly, sexy, daring, and dangerous. God's Word would have us be strong and "put on the whole armor of God" in order to resist the temptations of the world.

Questions

1. *What did Ruth, Esther, Sarah, and Rebekah have in common?*

2. *What was wrong with the "strange woman" Solomon described in Proverbs 5 and 6?*

3. *What qualities should a young person look for when seeking out friends of the opposite sex?*

7. Finding the Right Girl

You probably will one day select your own wife or husband. So, now as a teen-ager, you ought to be deciding what kind of mate you want.

It's hard enough to get the right mate for yourself; to pick out a mate for somebody else, wow, you *really* had better be prayed-up! The servant of Abraham (Gen. 24:7) was sent out to get a bride for his son, Isaac. The girls in those days did not have much to do with selecting their own husbands and sometimes neither did the boys in selecting a wife. There are some lessons to learn from this unusual love story.

You've heard of blind dates. This one might well be called a blind wedding! Under the Levitical law the dedicated Jewish priest could not have just anybody for a wife. So God commanded, "And he shall take a wife in her virginity. A widow or a divorced woman, or profane, or an harlot, these shall he not take: but he shall take a virgin of his own people to wife" (Lev. 21:13–14).

Isaac was not to have just anybody. Rebekah was a virgin. She had not known man (Gen. 24:16). She had kept herself pure for the man she would one day marry. This is as it should be! "Who can find a virtuous woman?" (Prov. 31).

This should be our determination. Girls,

remember there are many guys who want a virtuous bride. And young men don't want to marry someone who is "second-hand," who has been pawed over and mauled by other boys before she got around to you. "Keep thyself pure," the Bible instructs us.

Rebekah was "very fair." It is natural to fall for a girl, or a guy, who is most attractive to you. But remember, "beauty is only skin deep," and you need to find a girl who has something in her head and in her heart—not just in her face and form. She ought to be attractive to *you;* she does *not* have to be attractive to every other boy in your school or church.

Not only was Rebekah pure and fair, but she was industrious. She was not afraid of work. She was carrying the buckets to the well for water. Doing her duty. You'll be smart to find a girl who knows her way around the kitchen and is interested in cooking, homemaking, and serving. You and your children are going to need that kind of a girl. Today many a young woman has a career, pleasure, and dollar signs in front of her eyes; such modern gold diggers will sadly disappoint a young man who wants a real wife to make a happy home!

Rebekah was generous. She shared the refreshing well water with this stranger. Don't fall for a selfish girl. Rebekah was hospitable, inviting the man to her home to meet her parents, and letting him know that there was a guest room available (Gen. 24:25).

Rebekah also was spiritually minded, for when she saw that the man worshipped the Lord and that he was in the will of the Lord, she "ran and told them of her mother's house these things."

There is no reason to believe that Rebekah was concerned about the riches of Isaac, but when she did what she ought to do, she ended up with expensive earrings and bracelets. She did not marry for money, but "being in the way" of the Lord, she had all that she needed. The main thing is to be in the will of God, and God will provide all of the "things" that we need (Matt. 6:33).

Rebekah was decisive. When her parents and older brother tried to get her to postpone the wedding, she said, "I will go." There was no beating around the bush. Her mind was made up. It was a big step of faith, but she knew that it was of the Lord. Today God would have a person know about the one they are to marry, and if *God* is in it, it will work out just right.

We can be sure about the "good, and acceptable, and perfect, will of God" for our life (Rom. 12:1–2).

Questions

1. How can this romantic episode be called a blind wedding?

2. What are some of the desirable qualities of Rebekah?

3. What are some indications that Rebekah was spiritually minded?

8. Boys and Girls Are Different

Under the Mosaic law a woman was not to wear that which pertaineth unto a man (Deut. 22:5). God made men and women different, and He wants to keep it that way.

The unisex idea is not of God. God would have girls to be dainty, sweet, lovely, and feminine. He wants boys to be real boys—not half-girl or effeminate wimps.

When I was a young man, the only women you would ever see wearing men's clothes in public would be women of the street. The cheap harlot or dance hall floozy might so dress. The only possible exception would have been farm women or others who had outdoor work to do in bad weather. Even then, they would dress like a lady when they went out in public.

Then came World War II, and many women went to work for the first time in war plants. Rosie the Riveter became a symbol of the tough, man-like female as she donned man's trousers and began to smoke, talk, curse, and dress like men. A preacher made this colorful comment: "When the American mother stalked out of her home wearing men's britches, with a cigarette in her mouth and a flask of whiskey on her hip, and went out to dance with other women's husbands until

4:00 A.M., we were hit by something more deadly than German bullets!"

By the late sixties, many women picked up this un-Scriptural habit of dressing like men. Then the Beatles came over from England with their mop-top haircuts and boys began to wear long hair, and we were in the hippie era, in which it was often impossible to tell the boys from the girls.

We began to hear more and more about unisex and homosexuals. Even nature itself tells us it is a shame for a man to have long hair! (1 Cor. 11:14)

God made the sexes different for definite purposes. He wants girls to be feminine and boys to be masculine. The girl's hair should be long enough to definitely identify her as a girl and a boy's should be short enough that there is never any doubt that he is a boy! A woman's hair is her covering and her long hair is her glory (1 Cor. 11:15).

Boys are not to be "effeminate" or "abusers of themselves with mankind" (1 Cor. 6:9) any more than they are to be guilty of fornication or idolatry.

When people honor God and believe the Bible, it is understood that the boy is to be the aggressor in the courtship relationship. It is considered improper for the girl to "chase" the boy. Most boys like a girl who is feminine and certainly most of them become wary of a girl who is too forward or aggressive. Most boys do not like for a girl to call them up nor to act bold in her desire for a date. Many a girl has lost a boy's interest by being too forward.

Girls need to remember, too, that boys are more easily aroused than girls and many times are inclined to have sex on their minds even when the girl doesn't realize it. For this reason girls need to be modest and be careful not to lead a boy on or become too affectionate. Girls need to be careful how they walk, talk, and touch, as well as how they dress.

Boys should determine to always be a gentleman around members of the opposite sex. Boys should guard their talk around girls just like they would around their mother. They should act as decent around girls as they would want other boys to be with their own sister.

In Israel a virtuous girl was protected by her parents who were expected to be able to give proof that she was still a virgin, in case her husband had doubts after they were married (Deut. 22). Under the Mosaic law, if the girl *did* prove not to be virtuous, the people could take her out and stone her to death. If an evil man had forced himself upon her (raped her), however, the girl was to be spared and pitied. But the man who assaulted her was to die. If this law were still carried out, there would be very few rape stories on the evening news!

Questions

1. *Give some reasons why girls should not chase after boys.*

2. *Why should a girl be proper and modest around boys?*

3. *What are the dangers of flirting and care less- ness in a girl's dress and deportment?*

LOVE AND SEX

9. The Story of Birth

The story of birth is most amazing because it is the God-appointed means of bringing a living being into this world. Any young person reading the Bible for the first time will be struck by how often such verses about birth occur: "Isaac entreated the Lord for his wife, because she was barren (she had been unable to have children): and the Lord was entreated of him, and Rebekah his wife conceived" (Gen. 25:21). The Lord heard Isaac's prayer and sent not just a baby but twins, after Rebekah conceived. They had been unable to have a baby until they prayed about it. Then they came together again and soon "the children struggled together within her." There were twins in her womb and later Esau and Jacob, one after the other, were born.

Where do babies come from? They ulti-mately come from *God*, as all life comes from Him.

Jacob explains who is with him in the returning throng and says they are "the children which God hath graciously given thy servant" (Gen. 33:5). He knew God had given him these children. Thus sex, conception, and birth are interrelated in God's plan for mankind.

Genesis 3:16 tells us that because of sin in the human race, women will conceive and bear children "in sorrow" (there will be pain and travail in the birth of a baby), and because of woman's rebellion, the wife will be ruled by her husband (or submissive to her husband, as Paul explains in Eph. 5:22).

Genesis 20:18 tells of a time when "the Lord had fast closed up all the wombs of the house of Abimelech," so you can see that God has the final say-so about whether a child is conceived or not. Rachel was "in hard labor," so much so that she died, as Benjamin was born (Gen. 35). This is part of the "sorrow" of childbirth. Any young girl who thinks it would be exciting and "fun" to have a baby needs to realize that "as soon as Zion travailed, she brought forth her children" (Isa. 66:8). The pain and anguish of childbirth is no joke. It is rightly called "travail" (Ps. 48:6). Travail is great pain, sometimes agony!

God provides the life, knows all about the baby while it is being carried in the womb by its mother, and ordains what that child should do or be when it is grown. This we know from Jeremiah 1:5, "Before I formed thee in the belly I knew thee; and before thou camest forth out of the womb I sanctified thee, and I ordained thee a prophet unto the nations." From this, among other things, you can see the terrible crime of abortion. We see also that God has a plan for your life after you are born, but He knows all about it before you are born.

Questions

1. Twins were born to Rebekah who previously had been _____.

2. Jacob realized and testified that his children had come from _____.

3. What does "travail" mean?

4. When had God ordained Jeremiah?

10. Naming the Baby

"A good name is rather to be chosen than great riches" (Prov. 22:1) and "A good name is better than precious ointment" (Eccles. 7:1). Names mean something to God. He commands that we not take His name in vain (Ex. 20:7).

Today people usually name the baby for someone in the family, or people select the name of some famous TV or movie star because it sounds modern and popular.

Usually in the Bible a baby was named with something very definite in mind. Joseph in the Bible means "adding." He was added to the many sons of Jacob. Joseph was in many remarkable ways a type of Christ; that is, there was much in the life of Joseph that was like Christ. Some writers have referred to Jesus as our heavenly Joseph or as our heavenly Joshua. So names meant something in the Bible.

When Joseph interpreted the dream of Pharaoh and then was selected to be the governor of the land, the great potentate gave Joseph another name meaning "a revealer of secret things" Gen. 41.

When Joseph married and had two sons, he named one Manasseh (meaning "forgetting"), for he said, "God . . . hath made me forget all my toil"

(Gen. 41:51). When his second son was born, he called him Ephraim (meaning "fruitful"), for he said, "God hath caused me to be fruitful in the land of my affliction" (Gen. 41:52).

Have you ever sought to find out what *your* name means? Your last name is your family name. When I was going out with other young people, my Dad used to say, "Remember whose boy you are." I'm glad now that I can look back and realize that I never did disgrace his name or break the heart of my parents by sinful foolishness. When we are a Christian, we also carry the name of God with us. How much more should we never want to hurt the name of Christ. Read 2 Tim. 2:19.

Questions

1. *What did Solomon say a good name was better than?*

2. *Why should Christians, especially, keep their names untarnished?*

11. Good Grief!

"And Esau was forty years old when he took to wife Judith . . . which was a grief of mind unto Isaac and to Rebekah" (Gen. 26:34–35). Why did Esau want to break the heart of his parents? Because Esau was carnal, he was a rebel; he had his mind on the fleshly and material things of this world. So it is not surprising that when he took a wife, it was someone like Judith. He had already despised his birthright, having sold that honor for a "mess of pottage" (a serving of red beans).

Samson, the strong man in the Bible, started his downfall when he brought "grief" to his parents by demanding that he be permitted to marry a Philistine girl. He disregarded his parents' wisdom. And Samson let the flesh rule his life. He just *had* to have that appealing woman. So one of the most interesting characters in all the Bible had his life cut short because of sex sins. Ultimately he lost his strength, his power, his testimony, his eyesight, and finally his life. Violating God's word in sex matters always brings grief.

The young man in Proverbs who followed an enticing young adulteress to her perfumed paradise was like an ox going to the slaughter (Prov. 7:22). What grief he brought upon himself and others! One cannot take fire in his bosom without being burned (Prov. 6:27).

Instead of bringing grief to your own life and to the hearts of your parents, why not give grief to the Devil by staying pure and by thus also inspiring other young people to do the same? There will be others who will follow your right example and thus save themselves many years of grief.

Questions

1. *Why was Esau not likely to choose the right kind of wife?*

2. *How could Samson have saved himself grief?*

3. *The only "good grief" is that which you give to the Devil. Can you think of one way to do this?*

Love and Sex
12. Are Not the Same

We hear much about "making love" from those who know little or nothing about true love. "Love is of God; and every one that loveth is born of God, and knoweth God . . . God is love" (1 John 4:7–8).

To many people, "making love" is something dirty and evil, with intimate embraces and indulgences on the part of a couple who may know very little, if anything at all, about real love. True love and sex are not necessarily the same thing.

"Thou shalt not follow a multitude to do evil," God warns in Ex. 23:2. Because "everybody's doing it" does not make it right; and even if everyone else is doing wrong, that is no reason for *you* to.

Married people in love enjoy the intimacy of the marriage embrace. Their kisses are real and meaningful. But to a great host of single people, kissing and embracing are just a lustful means of temporarily satisfying carnal desires which have been aroused by looking at lewd pictures, listening to dirty music, or pawing one another in a darkened room or automobile.

While sex and love are not the same, it is true that married people in love do enjoy the kind of thrilling and wonderful sex life that most young people know nothing about. It is also true that many couples who "mess around" with sex or handle forbidden fruit of sex are not in love at all.

Jacob, who worked 14 years to win his wife, Rachel, was really in love! Rebekah fell in love with Isaac from what she had heard and seen of him even before she met him. The love match was of God (Gen. 24:58; 29:20).

Ruth fell in love with Boaz, and he with her. They took time to make sure. The romance was of God. It was true love (Ruth 2).

God tells us in Ephesians 5 that a man should love his wife as much as Christ loved the church—which means he would be willing to be crucified for her.

In Proverbs 7, "Let us take our fill of love until the morning" is not really talking about the true kind of love. Rather, it pictures an evil and lustful woman enticing a young man to lead him to "slaughter" just like an old dumb ox. Soon he would be "cast down" and "slain by her," and he would find that "her house is the way to hell, going down to the chambers of death"! The things that are pure, right, and holy in his life will be killed, and his life will be filled with evil, corruption, and disappointment.

No, sex and love are not the same thing.

Questions

1. How much did God say a man should love his wife?

2. How is a young man's involvement with lust like a dumb ox?

13. Sexual Temptation— How to Handle It!

Joseph was a handsome, charming, and very intelligent young man. Remember his dreams and how his brothers hated him for them. They also resented the fact that his father seemed to favor Joseph over the other brothers and had given him the beautiful coat of many colors (Gen. 37:3). They were a jealous lot, these older brothers of Joseph. So they cast him into a pit to die, later deciding to sell him as a slave to Midianitish merchantmen who took him down to Egypt and offered him on the auction block to the highest bidder.

Joseph became a slave to Potiphar who soon made him the superintendent of all his estate. Potiphar was a wealthy land owner whose work sometimes took him on long journeys elsewhere. Joseph—brilliant, responsible, and wise—took care of everything. Well, almost everything.

While Potiphar was a man of diligence and integrity, he was married to a woman whose moral standards left much to be desired. Though she was married to a successful man, she decided to make a play for Joseph and have her a "lover" on the side. She "cast her eyes upon Joseph" (Gen. 39:7), and attempted to lead him off into sexual sin.

Joseph cried, "How then can I do this great wickedness, and sin against God?" Joseph knew that if no one else was looking that *God* was, and he refused her and darted from the house and her presence.

You had better make up your mind to it, sooner or later you, too, will be tempted to do something morally wrong. What will you do? How will you overcome it? Is there a way out?

God says, "Resist the devil, and he will flee from you" (James 4:7). He admonishes us to "put on the whole armor of God" (Eph. 6), and insists "keep thyself pure" (1 Tim. 5:22).

How can we do it? What do you do with sexual temptation? Let's see what Joseph did in Genesis 39.

He knew that the Lord had prospered him. It is always very good to look back and see what God has done for you. Joseph wanted God to be close to him; we must "draw nigh to God," if we want Him to "draw nigh to us" (see James 4:8). It is important to stay close to God for strength and blessing.

Joseph had a testimony with his master. His master (Potiphar) saw that God was with Joseph. In other words Joseph so lived before Potiphar that the wealthy landowner knew that Joseph was God's servant. We are to let our lights shine before men (Matt. 5:16). Joseph did not want to ruin his testimony with Potiphar, which he certainly would have done, if he had given in to this sexual sin.

Joseph was busy. He had his hands full. He was "overseer" of Potiphar's house and estate, even "all that he had." Staying busy helps us stay out of trouble, for idleness is always "the devil's workshop."

Potiphar was depending upon Joseph. He had so trusted Joseph that he did not even know what his possessions were—except "the bread which he did eat" (Gen. 39:6). The fact that his master had so much faith in Joseph helped Joseph to take his stand. Remember, there are those who are counting on you. You never want to disappoint your parents, pastor, schoolmates, and others who have confidence in you.

These are some of the things that kept Joseph true and pure. Since he was close to God, we can be sure that he prayed every day. So when the big crisis came, and the alluring and beautiful young woman threw herself at him, he was able to resist. Joseph did this without even having a Bible to read.

David could say, "Thy *Word* have I hid in mine heart, that I might not sin against thee" (Ps. 119:11). We have the Word of God to give us strength and help in time of temptation.

Questions

1. How did Joseph happen to be sold as a slave?

2. Why did Joseph not give in to sin when temptation came?

3. What do we have to help us that Joseph did not have?

SEX AND THE SCARLET SIN

14. The Scarlet Sin

"Thou shalt not commit adultery" is one of the ten commandments that God gave to the human race for its good (Ex. 20:14). A loving God repeats this in Deut. 5:18 because he wants people not to miss this important command. Adultery is the tragic sin of sexual indulgence with someone other than one's own husband or wife. It is always wrong—never right under any circumstance.

This is called the scarlet sin. On the part of single people it is generally called fornication, but it is the same sin—sexual immorality. It can often begin with a look or a touch. Then caressing, fondling, and petting can suddenly project the couple into such terrible desire that they are led into the scarlet sin. Television makes adultery or fornication look all right, and Hollywood glorifies it. But millions of hearts and lives have been broken because of this sin. Adultery leads to shame, never to happiness as modern TV writers and novelists would lead one to think.

God knows what He is talking about when He commands, "thou shalt not covet thy neighbour's wife" (Ex. 20:17). Coveting a person that you do not have the right to, is often the result of looking, longing, and lusting. So God tells young people, "Let thine eyes look right on, and let thine eyelids look straight before thee" (Prov. 4:25). Looking often leads to longing. That's why Jesus said, "whosoever looketh on a woman to lust after her hath committed adultery with her already in his heart" (Matt. 5:28).

Adultery breaks up marriages, destroys lives, leads to dismay, disappointment, distress, and frequently to disease and death. "The wages of sin is death," Paul writes in Romans. Stay out of sexual sins!

Fornication and adultery are among the sins that Jesus said "cometh out of the heart" of depraved human beings. These are "evil things" from within that "defile the man" (Mark 7:20–23).

Jesus forgave the woman "taken in adultery" in John 8, but He told her to "go, and sin no more."

Paul said that people of the world are "filled with all unrighteousness, fornication," among other vile sins (Rom. 1:29). That's why some people talk dirty and blurt out filthy jokes at every opportunity, for they are "filled" with these things.

God tells us that the scarlet sins of adultery and fornication are the "works of the flesh," and that they who do such things shall not inherit the kingdom of God (Gal. 5:19).

Wise young people will purpose in their hearts to never be tripped and trapped by the scarlet sin!

Questions

1. Can you distinguish between fornication and adultery since both are the "scarlet sin?"

2. List some of the dire consequences of the scarlet sin.

3. Can sexual sins be forgiven?

4. Why are some people constantly speaking evil and making jokes about sexual sins?

15. Sexually Transmitted Diseases

A teen-ager who fools around and does things that are sexually dirty or immoral might end up with a terrible disease. There was a time when young Americans going into the armed services were shown films that would shock and sicken them. These films were graphic medical movies made to frighten young men and keep them from wanting to get sexually involved with anyone before they married. Those who did get involved often ended up with a terrible venereal disease (VD), or as it is called today sexually transmitted disease (STD). Today, as many as 30 million Americans are plagued with such diseases, with the greatest increase being among teen-agers and those in their twenties.

Sometimes diseases are brought upon people because of their sins. God told His people, "If thou wilt diligently hearken to the voice of the Lord thy God, and wilt do that which is right in his sight, and wilt give ear to his commandments, and keep all his statutes, I will put NONE OF THESE DISEASES upon thee, which I have brought upon the Egyptians" (Ex. 15:26). Fear of disease as well as the fear of an unwanted pregnancy has kept many a young person from committing the scarlet sin of adultery.

It pays to stay pure and do right by saying "no" to sexual sins. God said to His children, "And the Lord will take away from thee all sickness, and will put none of the evil diseases of Egypt, which thou knowest, upon thee; but will lay them upon all them that hate thee" (Deut. 7:15).

Sin brings heartache, misery, and mental anguish in many psychological ways as well as physical disease. There were earlier forms of VD that were accompanied with terrible pain and weakness, long before herpes and AIDS were on the scene.

Yes, the scarlet sin can bring sorrow and grief. Proud, arrogant friends may talk you into something, but David found that when his foot slipped, such friends magnified themselves against him. Those friends will let you down just when you need them if you insist on having that kind of friends.

Herpes is a terrible disease today when it affects the private parts of the body. Once there, doctors have found that there is no cure and that the pain and sores will be recurrent throughout life.

Some people have contracted herpes accidentally and innocently, but it started out as a sex disease, especially among those who lived in sin and thought they could indulge in the secret delights of married love without being married.

Also, many a married person, who committed adultery, has taken this awful and painful disease home to an innocent husband or wife.

Recently AIDS (Acquired Immune Deficiency Syndrome) has come on the scene. In America (as in most countries) the disease started among the homosexuals, whom the Bible calls sodomites. Sodomites attempt to satisfy their sexual desires with members of their own sex (Rom. 1:26–28). According to the Bible these are perverted people who go after "strange flesh" (Jude 7). They are called "filthy dreamers" in Jude 8, and will suffer the vengeance of eternal fire unless, of course, they are saved from this perversion.

In these last days before the return of the Lord, sodomites are increasing in number and in boldness. It is becoming again as it was in Genesis 19, when God, because He cannot stand this horrible sin of homosexuality, visited Sodom and Gomorrah with the judgment of fire and brimstone, literally blasting those ancient cities off the face of the earth and destroying everybody who lived there in a great holocaust.

God is merciful. He gives "space to repent." So in these last days, He has visited lands that have many sodomites with a new and horrible plague or pestilence called AIDS. The disease is worse than other forms of VD (like syphilis or herpes) because, as far as we know, it is not only incurable but fatal! Tens of thousands of the victims have and are dying in Africa from AIDS. Haiti (where there has been much homosexuality) has also been greatly stricken. Now the United States and other enlightened countries are also counting the dead in the many thousands.

Movie stars, rock musicians, TV personalities, and many, many people in the arts and fashion world have been stricken. As the homosexuals have come "out of the closet" (as they put it) and are marching, protesting, and demanding that their wicked and perverse life styles be accepted, more and more of them have been stricken with AIDS.

You need to make up your mind now that you will never play around with the sin of sodomy! "Keep thyself pure," God demands in the Scriptures. "Touch not the unclean thing," He adds. Never allow anyone to entice you into illicit sex situations or experimentation. "If sinners entice thee, consent thou *not!* " (Prov. 1:10)

Questions

1. Why did the army in former days show sickening films to scare the new soldiers?

2. How did God tell Israel they could avoid many diseases?

3. What sexual life style is most affected with the AIDS epidemic?

16. Dancing and Sex

When Moses brought the Ten Commandments down from the Mount, he found the people of Israel shouting and making a great noise. There was music, but to the man of God, it did not sound like good music (Ex. 32:18, 19).

Coming into the camp, Moses saw everyone dancing around an idolatrous golden calf they had made. This dancing around the golden calf was a symbol of their giving themselves to another god other than the true God. The music was wild and noisy, and as they danced—they were naked!

Pagan natives around heathen campfires often drink and dance until they become so aroused that they take off their clothes. Things haven't changed much in the dance of modern times. Young people dance in such a lewd and provocative manner that the flesh (sex lust) is aroused. They sway and writhe in front of each other in lustful movements. Many times they have very little clothing on, or the clothing is so tight that it is suggestive and revealing.

Rock stars have often been arrested for exposing themselves in a shameful manner while performing their heathen rituals with dirty lyrics and movements that are vile and lewd.

Almost always beer, wine, or liquor is served (or brought in) where there is dancing. Intoxication and dancing usually go hand in hand. On rare occasions there may be some well-chaperoned dances for young teens where there is no drinking, but just wait around a few years (maybe only a few months), and many of these same young people will be dancing where there is plenty of alcohol flowing.

The earlier years of dancing, especially for young girls, may be indeed quite innocent. Girls often say, "I can dance without having my mind on sex or something dirty." However, boys in most cases are thinking about something entirely different than these young girls are.

The dance and sex have always gone together. Some good Christian men met at prom time, in a city where I pastored, to try to convince school authorities that they should have a fine banquet with clean entertainment for the high school youth who didn't dance. For years this was done. These businessmen who had been saved in later years all testified that they had tasted liquor and raw sex for the first time at the annual high school prom.

The embrace of the dance, the closeness of the bodies (or the constant twisting, shaking, and writhing of the bodies) cannot but arouse a person and the dancing partner. The body's response to this type of physical stimulus is normal—but not designed to occur outside the marriage relationship.

David with the joy and excitement, similar to a young child on Christmas morning, danced with all his might in a celebration of ecstasy because of the Lord's blessing and the return of the Ark of the Covenant (2 Sam. 6:14). This is far different from modern dancing. It is also true that some forms of dancing are not as dirty and lustful as other forms. The ballet, for instance, is not always as suggestive and arousing as are other forms of dancing. Ballroom dancing is not as suggestive of the sex act as many of the dirty dances that have originated in recent years; however, often the evening gowns in ballroom dancing are skimpy, sensual, and revealing. The waltz is not as sensual as rock 'n' roll dances. The fox trot was not as sexy as the dancing of today.

It is impossible to separate sex and the dance; to a greater or lesser degree they go together. John the Baptist, the great preacher of Jesus' day, was beheaded after a lewd dance. After wicked King Herod witnessed a suggestive dance performed by the young girl Salome, he was inspired to give her anything she wanted as a result of her enticing dance (Matt. 14:6–10). It was her dancing that turned King Herod into a fiend.

In describing the prosperity of the wicked, God said among other things, "They send forth their little ones like a flock, and their children dance" (Job 21:11).

Evil men had burned the town of Ziklag and had kidnapped members of David's family (1 Sam. 30). It had been a terrible experience. When David finally found the wicked renegades who had perpetrated the crime, they "were spread abroad upon all the earth, eating and drinking, and dancing." Riotous celebration almost always includes dancing. This is one reason why crimes (often sex crimes) are committed at rock concerts.

In describing the works of the flesh, "revellings, and such like," are listed along with adultery, fornication, uncleanness, murders, and drunkenness. These "revellings" refer to drinking wine and dancing to pagan music. God mentions that "they which do such things shall not inherit the kingdom of God" (Gal. 5:21).

Dancing is worldly; it is sensual, suggestive, and arouses beastly appetites. It is almost always associated with drinking (often drugs) and a profane and corrupt atmosphere where the music is wild and Satanic. That should not only reveal to the honest Christian that dancing is off-limits to the believer, but should show the definite relationship the Bible teaches about dancing and sex.

Questions

1. How are modern dances much like heathen, tribal dances?

2. What do you learn about the dance from the atmosphere, drinks, and language there?

3. What did King Herod do to John the Baptist after a dance?

17. The Nakedness Question

God put fur on animals, scales on fish, and feathers on birds. When Adam and Eve in the garden realized they had sinned before God, they were embarrassed about their nakedness, and God made coats of skin to cover them. But, even before "the coats," the first couple had covered up with "fig leaves." And in the garden of Eden, God gave man his first clothes and expected human beings to cover themselves. So when the maniac of Gadara got rid of his demons (Mark 5) and Jesus came into his life, he was found sitting, "and clothed," and in his right mind. People in their right minds know that they should have on clothes.

It is true that in backward countries, the more pagan the heathen tribe the less clothing they usually wear. Missionaries tell us that as soon as these pagans get saved, they want to cover up their nakedness—they look for some clothing to put on. It may take awhile to teach them just how to dress and how much to cover up, but they soon learn.

God has a lot to say about nakedness. In Leviticus 18, the whole chapter deals with nakedness, He emphasizes again and again the danger of being careless about covering up. He plainly declares that we are not to uncover the nakedness of "any that is near of kin." So we are not to run around the house naked nor become immodest in other ways, even around our own family members and relatives.

Nudists boast that it is "healthy" to go without clothes and that people soon get used to it and think nothing of it, but God says that we are not to look upon the nakedness of other members of the family. This includes brothers, sisters, and in-laws.

God warns about living in sin with anyone—that is, exposing the body to anyone other than one's own wife or husband (Lev. 18:20).

God continues by talking about the terrible abominations of indulging in any kind of sexual union with one of the same sex (Lev. 18:22). This today is called homosexuality, but God referred to them as sodomites; it is perversion of the worst kind. Closely associated with this homosexual vice was the horrible and pagan custom of lying with animals. Evidently some nations had men who did this, and God said the land was defiled because of it, (Lev. 18:24, 25) and because of this the "land itself had vomited out her inhabitants." So none of these terrible abominations are ever to be considered. Don't even talk about it with anyone. God put it in Scripture with a strong warning!

In Leviticus 20:10–21, God again deals with nakedness, adultery, and homosexuality, and tells us that those who commit such sins should be put to death.

In Exodus 32:25 it was the nakedness of the people as much as anything else that brought the judgment of God and brought "shame" to them before their enemies.

Even so today, the enemies of the Lord look at immodest and improperly clad Christians, and the Christian testimony is put to shame. Christian girls and women should be careful not to dress in sensually provocative clothes (such as shorts, miniskirts, long-slit or open skirts, low-neck dresses, skimpy bathing suits, etc.) when they are around other people, for they thus bring shame and criticism to the Christian cause. They may also cause men to lust after them with evil thoughts. Many a woman or girl who has been assaulted (raped) or beaten and abused by some evil man has at least been partly to blame if she was dressed in such an immodest way as to cause temptation.

Men are easily aroused by what they see. Pornographic movie makers and dirty-book writers know this. The woman who first introduced the miniskirt said that now women of the world could announce that they were available for illicit sex in the afternoon! So we can see what some men think about when girls or women wear skimpy, suggestive attire.

Let "women adorn themselves in modest apparel" (1 Tim. 2:9). Some dresses are not modest; shorts that come way up above the knees are not modest; many bathing suits are not modest. If it be argued that the girl cannot find modest clothing, then she could have her mother or a seamstress make her modest clothing. At least, she can wear a robe to the water's edge to swim and then cover up properly when coming out of the water. If possible, go to a secluded spot on the ocean, gulf, or lake, and swim with just your own family; even then we should be modest. The family that has their own pool has another solution. Many good Christian camps have separate swim periods for boys and girls for these reasons.

Questions

1. *What do we learn from the maniac of Gadara? From heathen tribes?*

2. What did God make for Adam and Eve?

3. Under the Old Testament law, what happened to the person found guilty of adultery or homosexuality?

4. Why should Christian girls, especially, be careful about modesty?

18. Sex for Money

In finding out what the Bible teaches about sex, it is necessary to see what God says about harlots and whoredom. This idea of sex for money is a terrible sin, an awful crime against God and against humanity.

Don't let Hollywood or TV fool you as they laugh about such matters. They may call these women "hookers" or "call girls," but God calls them "whores" and "harlots." Again, this is private information which God gives us. It is not for public discussion, but we need to know how God frowns upon such things.

God warns parents not to let their daughters get into such terrible sin, saying that this could cause the whole land to fall into whoredom (Lev. 19:29). A whole nation can be corrupted with such vice. Entire civilizations have fallen when the people became obsessed with sexual vice and immorality, and it can start with girls becoming prostitutes or harlots.

We see the awful sin that Israel fell into when their people began to commit whoredom—patronizing harlots—which eventually led to idolatry and devil worship. The "anger of the Lord" was kindled against them because of this sin (Num. 25:1-3). No whore (immoral girl who gives herself for sex) nor any sodomite (homosexual) was ever to be tolerated among God's people (Deut. 23:17).

Harlots can be saved if they truly repent and turn to the Lord. The harlot Rahab (who had probably never known any other vocation) came to believe in the Lord and trust the servants of God so much that she was used of God to save the spies that Israel had sent to Jericho, and later Rahab became the (human) savior of all her household (Josh. 2).

Questions

1. What is a harlot?

2. How can an entire civilization crumble from within?

19. Dirty Pictures

When God's people (the children of Israel) passed over the Jordan River and into the promised land, God told them to drive out the idolatrous inhabitants of the land and destroy their pictures and their images (Num. 33:52). Why the pictures? What kind of pictures did those unsaved pagans have? They had wicked, vile pictures of sexual vice, perversion, and images of their heathen idols.

Pornography may be dirty and obscene words, or it may be lewd and immoral pictures—or both. Wherever the police arrest sex offenders after some terrible crime, they almost always find dirty, vulgar pictures. There are dirty magazines that no Christian should read or even look at. These evil, dirty picture magazines are floating around everywhere. Many of them, we are told, have to do with unnatural sex, perversion, and other licentious and vulgar things. Beware of such!

The "eye gate" is a powerful tool of Satan. The Devil made Eve see that the tree of forbidden fruit was "pleasant to the eyes" (Gen. 3:6). Pictures are fascinating. Little children are first attracted to colorful pictures long before they can read words. Television became an addiction to millions of people because they could finally "see" what they had been only hearing on radio. *Color* television made it all the more glamorous and appealing.

TV programming is becoming more and more suggestive and dirty. You can expect unsaved pagans to produce such programs, but we do not have to look at them.

The VCR machine can record things that are worthwhile; it makes it possible for people with TV sets to be more selective and watch things that are decent and proper at a later time. But Satan is fiendishly clever. He also has inspired the making of dirty videos and films that are profane, violent, sadistic, and adulterous. You will be tempted to watch dirty films with other young people. Unsaved adults, also, often make a play for young people by first showing them dirty movies. God says, "whatsoever things are pure . . . think on these things" (Phil. 4:8).

The man after God's own heart cried, "I will set no wicked thing before mine eyes" (Ps. 101:3). "The lust of the eyes" proves to be one of the best tools of Satan (1 John 2:16).

What kind of pictures did God want those Canaan-bound Israelites to destroy? Perhaps there was a connection between the pictures and the images since God mentions both in the same verse. Images were something they worshiped and revered. Today many people practically "worship" their movie idols and rock stars.

What kind of pictures do you have on the walls of your room? It is good to have pictures of family members and missionaries for whom you pray. The picture of an athlete, if he or she is a good Christian or a person of real character, is fine. Pictures of beautiful scenery, animal life, or other scenes showing the handiwork of God is appropriate for the walls of our homes—the flowers, mountains, rivers, and lakes all "declare the glory of God" (Ps. 19:1).

It hurts your Christian testimony to have photos of movie or rock stars on your walls. It also is bad for your own eyes and heart, for too often we find that our hearts follow our eyes (Job 31:7).

God told those Israelites that if they would not drive out the inhabitants of the land, those heathen who remained would be pricks in their eyes and thorns in their sides to vex and aggravate them (Num. 33:55, 56). In fact, God says that if they embraced the sins of the heathen, what was planned for the heathen would be done to them. So if we embrace the sins of the worldlings, we'll have done to *us* what God had planned to do to *them!*

The best way to keep yourself pure and clean in mind and thought is to keep your eyes where they belong. Don't let Satan's pictures get to you!

Questions

1. Why did God want the Israelites to get rid of those pictures before they could enjoy the beauty and bounty of the promised land?

2. Are there some pictures you ought to dispose of? Something that maybe you've hoped your parents would never find?

WHEN GIANTS FALL

20. Don't Marry a Pagan!

It is always best to select your close friends, or your dates, from people who are in God's family. God forbids a saved person to marry an unsaved person. Be not unequally yoked together with unbelievers (2 Cor. 6:14). The person with whom you are friends today may be the person you marry tomorrow.

The Israelite father or mother was never to permit their children to "make marriages" with the pagans around them (Deut. 7:3–4), because the unsaved partner would turn the believer away from God to "serve other gods," and thus the anger of the Lord would be kindled against the believer. The believer is never to marry "the inhabitants of the land" or the people of this world, for Christians belong to another world; our citizenship is in heaven (Phil. 3).

If you date an unsaved person, there is always the danger that you will fall in love and marry that unsaved person and bring great trouble and heartache upon your life. "What communion hath light with darkness?" God asks in 2 Cor. 6:14. Someday when you begin to look for a mate, look in your "own tribe." Don't date a pagan, and you'll not end up marrying a pagan.

God rebuked the intermarriage of the Jews with the heathen races among them, as they married wives of Ashdod, Ammon, and Moab (Neh. 13:23). They were reminded that the great and wise King Solomon had sinned by doing this very thing—taking heathen wives. It was the "outlandish women" that caused Solomon to sin.

God calls it "great evil" to transgress against God "in marrying *strange* wives" (Neh. 13:27). *Strange* means those you have no right to (and they are foreign to your way of thinking, talking, and acting). For a Christian to marry an unsaved person is outright disobedience to God and will cause only heartache, anguish, and marital problems. "Can two walk together, except they be agreed?" (Amos 3:3).

Often an unsaved boy will pretend to be a Christian just to win the girl who has caught his eye. Again, many an unsaved church member thinks he is saved and may not be, so you'd better be very careful. When you date a boy (or girl), make absolutely sure they are really saved before you make any kind of commitment to them.

This is another good reason never to become intimate or even affectionate with a boy or girl before marriage. When young people get involved in necking, kissing, and petting before marriage, it is awfully easy to get swept off your feet and think surely this has to be "real love." Then it is easy to rationalize and think that if God has let you truly fall in love like this, it must be His will to go on and get married even if he (or she) is not a Christian!

Questions

1. *Give two reasons why a Christian should not marry an unsaved person.*

2. *Why would God classify a fine, educated, well-dressed American young person as a heathen or pagan?*

3. *Why is it dangerous for a Christian to date one who is unsaved?*

21. Many Wives and Concubines

God warns against multiple wives, "Neither shall he multiply wives to himself" (Deut. 17:17). Solomon was ruined because of his many wives. David had many troubles partly because he had more than one wife. Samson was ruined by the women in his life.

The New Testament says that a deacon or a bishop (minister) should be "the husband of one wife" (1 Tim. 3). It is usually God's plan for a man to have a wife; it is *never* God's will for a man to have *more* than one wife.

Since this is true, it is vitally important to make sure you get the right wife the first time and then remember that it is "until death do you part."

Mormons and other religious cults have permitted a man to have two or more wives, sometimes under the same roof, which causes heartache, jealousy, and strife. Because of such problems, it is against the law in our nation to be a bigamist (have more than one wife).

Since God makes marriage a permanent thing and declares "what God hath joined together let not man put asunder," we know that divorce and remarriage to another is never in the plan of God.

Two questions often asked are, "What were concubines in the Bible?" and "Why were men permitted to have them?"

The dictionary describes a concubine as a woman who lives with a man without being married to him—a common law wife or mistress. A man and his concubine would be people who cohabit without being legally joined in matrimony. There is much of this unholy living going on today, to our shame.

While it is assumed that concubines were mistresses who were available to their masters, many of them were servants, and apparently many household chores were done by them. Often slave girls taken captive in battle were brought home by the men to be servants as well as concubines. King Solomon had 700 wives who were princesses (1 Kings 11:3) and 300 concubines! He had a large palace with many servants. The Bible says it was his wives who, later in his old age, turned away the great king's heart from the Lord. He had "strange wives" who worshiped strange gods, and this was what destroyed his greatness.

Was it God's will that the king have 700 wives and 300 concubines? Of course not! This was certainly his downfall. He was very wise in other matters, but very foolish and disobedient regarding wives. Solomon learned many things about women (as you may well imagine) and was used of God to give us some of the richest and wisest instruction in all Scripture about marriage, the home, and family. It was too bad that later in his own life he did not follow his own words of wisdom. Though concubines are mentioned in the Old Testament, it certainly does not mean that God approved of them.

In the New Testament, men are plainly told to be "the husband of one wife," if they marry. Jesus made it very clear that marriage is to last until death takes one of the partners and that adultery is such a terrible sin that it brings down the judgment of God (Heb. 13:4).

Questions

1. *What really caused the downfall of Solomon?*

22. The Playboy with a Hole in His Head

Sisera, who had the potential of being a great warrior, went out to battle against God's people. As captain of Jabin's army (Judg. 4:7, 13), Sisera had a tough reputation as a fighter, and "he had 900 chariots of iron." But when he met Israel's army, all of Sisera's men were slain, for God was blessing the forces of Deborah and Barak.

Sisera also had quite a reputation as a ladies' man. He thought any woman would be delighted to have him enter her tent. In fleeing from the heat of the battle, he fled to the tent of Jael, a married woman he knew. She was waiting for him, but not in the fashion he imagined.

He was exhausted and ready for sleep when she invited him to come in and rest, crying "turn in to me; fear not" (Judg. 4:18). She gave him a bottle of milk for strength, and he commanded her to stand at the door of the tent and watch for the enemy while he slept.

When he was sound asleep, she took a long nail, perhaps a tent spike, and with a big hammer drove it into his temple while he slept, fastening him to the ground. He was so weary and deep asleep that he never knew what hit him. Later Jael went out to meet Barak and led him to her trophy, the very dead captain Sisera!

Many a young person has been slain (morally and spiritually) by turning in to the wrong companions. "Turn in to me!" cried Jael. Sisera thus met his doom. Young person, remember, there will be many temptations along the way. Sometimes a friend may say to you, "turn in to me." Give that person a deaf ear as Joseph did. "A companion of fools shall be destroyed" (Prov. 13:20).

The beer, wine, and liquor crowd will cry, "turn in to me." The pornographic movie fiends will say, "turn in to me." Dirty book publishers and suggestive "girlie" magazines will try to lead you astray with their "turn in to me" line. Don't forget it and don't ever get so weary or off guard that you fall for their enticements. Read Proverbs 1:7–23.

Sisera, the playboy with a hole in his head, broke his mother's heart. She was waiting at home for her grown son to return from battle. But Jael had smitten him through his temples and then "smote off his head." Many a young person has, so to speak, "lost their head" when they didn't intend to. Sisera fell at the feet of this woman. If you "lose your head" and let some person make a fool of you—you, too, may end up lying at the feet of your adversary. Could it possibly be that Sisera was off guard partly because he was so tired and discouraged? When you get "down" and feel defeated, it is easy to give in to sin.

"The mother of Sisera looked out a window, and cried . . . why is his chariot so long in coming? why tarry the wheels of his chariot?" (Judg. 5:28). Her damsels replied in essence, "You know how he *is*. They have made a speedy conquest. Then they take the spoil and divide the prey. They will come home wearing beautiful colors of needlework, you know. And of course, the *girls!* Sisera will have a 'damsel or two' " (v. 30). They knew Sisera was a playboy who was loose with the opposite sex. His flair for the bold and brassy life finally finished him off.

Questions

1. *Name two reasons why Sisera was defeated and slain.*

2. *Why was his mother so worried?*

23. Samson—Sin Slays the Strong Man

God gave Samson unusual physical strength. Samson had godly parents; he must have had good upbringing. God brought him on the scene as the thirteenth judge of Israel to use him and to show forth God's power in him.

Remember, God wants to use *you*, too, and the Devil knows that if he can trip you and trap you with sexual temptation, he can get you sidetracked and ultimately destroy you and your usefulness to God. Samson is a good illustration of this.

It all began when Samson first went down to Timnath "and saw a woman" he just had to have. His parents warned him not to be so foolish, but Samson (like many a young Christian) thought he knew more than his parents. He just had to marry this heathen Philistine girl "for she pleaseth me well" (Judg. 14:3).

When we *must* please ourselves at any cost, we are on the way to a shattering experience.

Samson was so strong that he could tear apart the jaws of a lion with his bare hands. He caught 300 foxes and somehow tied their tails together and put firebrands between them in order to burn up the fields of the Philistines. By then his first marriage was broken up, for his wife that he "had to have" so badly had now become the wife of a "friend" of his. Things like this happen when people marry outside of the will of God.

Samson was strong enough to smite "hip and thigh" the enemies of the Lord, but he could not control his own desires and passion. Soon he was bound and tied by his enemies. Once more the power of the Lord came upon him, and his bonds were broken. Then he took the famous "jawbone of an ass" and slew a thousand of his enemies. What a slaughter!

By now Samson had tasted the forbidden fruits of the flesh, and we find him going to Gaza and spending time with a fallen woman—a harlot (Judg. 16). Sin is progressive. He would not have imagined when he first took that Philistine bride that he would one day actually be patronizing a paid prostitute. But he did! Sin has awful power when it is unleashed in our lives.

Still Samson was strong enough to walk off with the gate of the city, bars, posts, and all! Next he was captivated with the beautiful, enticing, and notorious Delilah. But he did not by now have sense enough to know that she was a toy in the hands of the brutal Philistines. She was setting Samson up so they could find where his great strength came from (Judg. 16:5).

She kept putting him to sleep after he continued to deceive her about his great strength. Each time he would wake up to defeat his enemies again by snapping the strange things they tied him with, just as if it had been a thread holding him.

His hair was his special mark of a Nazarite vow—identifying one who was set aside as a servant of God. He finally told Delilah that if he should be "shaven," he would be "weak . . . like any other man" (Judg. 16:17). Once more she teased and caressed him and got him to sleep with his head in her lap. He slept soundly. Those Philistine barbers were expert at handling the shears so quietly and deftly that they cut off his hair without waking him up. If that seems strange, remember that by now old Satan had him in a stupor of sin.

Samson thought he could get up as always and exert his great strength against his enemies. But this time he found himself weak like other men. "He wist not that the Lord was departed from him" (Judg. 16:20).

Soon the Philistines surrounded him and captured him. In horrible retribution for the tricks he had played on them, they gouged out his eyes. With the blood running down his face, they bound him with fetters of brass, and he was too weak to resist. This is what sin did to Samson, and it can do the same to you.

The strong man Samson was soon grinding in the prison house just like a beast of burden. His great strength came back only long enough for him to pull down a huge building upon himself and his enemies, so that "the dead which he slew at his death were more than they which he slew in his life" (Judg. 16:30).

Thus we can see how sexual sins can weaken and ruin even a person of great power and great influence. We need to be on guard all the time.

Questions

1. *Why was Satan especially anxious to get rid of Samson?*

2. *What was Samson's first big mistake that started him down hill?*

3. Some people fall because of greed, jealousy, or idolatry. What were some of the things that caused Samson to stumble?

4. Samson grinding in the prison house, with his eyes out, is a picture of what?

24. King David and Bathsheba

Pull down the shades! Surely Bathsheba, the beautiful wife of Uriah the Hittite, could have been careful to do her bathing behind walls, or at least see that her maidens had a screen in front of her.

David was now the mighty and popular King of Israel. He had won many battles. He was famous and wealthy. He had triumphed in the civil wars that rocked the land. David had several wives and many children by these wives (2 Sam. 3:2–5). It was not in the direct will of God for these Old Testament saints to have more than one wife, the New Testament clarifies that. And it surely added to their grief and heartache.

But the eye of man is never satisfied. Unless we constantly keep our eyes upon the Lord and stay busy for Him, the best of Christians can get into trouble. David proved this (2 Sam. 11).

While David's warriors had gone to battle, David "tarried still at Jerusalem." The Devil caught him off guard. He was weak and perhaps tired after all the wars and strife that had plagued his kingdom. A Christian needs to be exceptionally careful when weak, tired, or discouraged. On the other hand, some have fallen into their greatest temptation after a big victory when everything seems to be under control.

At any rate, when kings were going forth to battle, David was at home alone. He was restless one night and walked up on the flat rooftop of his home. From that vantage point he saw the beautiful Bathsheba "washing herself"; she was a very beautiful woman to look upon.

David sent for her and with her committed the terrible sin of adultery. The sordid result after it was all over was remorse. But tears, shame, and regret did not wipe the slate clean.

David tried to "cover up" his sin by getting rid of Bathsheba's husband, so he could legally have her as his wife. Unable to trick Uriah, David had him killed in battle by having his general put poor Uriah in the forefront of a hot battle and all the soldiers withdrawing from Uriah. Though it appeared to be a tragedy of battle, yet it was a deliberate murder in the eyes of God. So the sin of murder was added to the sin of adultery! One sin leads to another. Lying, deceit, and hatred often follow in the wake of such sins.

Nobody ever gets away with adultery, "Be sure your sin will find you out." God said to David, "Behold I will raise up evil against thee out of thine own house, and I will take thy wives before thine eyes, and give them unto thy neighbor" (2 Sam. 12:11, 12). "For thou didst it secretly: but I will do this thing before all Israel, and before the sun." David found that he had given occasion to the enemies of the Lord to blaspheme his God. David had hurt his testimony and had broken his wonderful fellowship with a holy God.

God did forgive David for his terrible sin, when he cried to God in true remorse and repentance (Ps. 51), but the sword never departed from David's house. What he sowed, he reaped; and David reaped devastating consequences. The son of David and Bathsheba died while an infant. Later there were terrible crimes committed against his own children—very similar to the kinds of sin David had committed. His son Absalom rebelled against David and tried to steal his kingdom away.

Of course, Bathsheba should have been more careful in bathing on her rooftop. How important it is for girls to be modest and have proper behavior. And boys should remember that Satan is waiting around hoping to pull the rug out from under them. Beware of the demon of lust!

Questions

1. *Suggest some reasons why David may have been vulnerable at this time.*

2. *How could Bathsheba have helped to avoid the tragedy?*

3. *How did David try to cover up his sin?*

4. *How is the law of sowing and reaping seen in this incidence?*

25. Doing Your Own Thing

The book of Judges ends with no king in Israel and "every man did that which was right in his own eyes" (Judg. 21:25). In other words, everybody was doing his own thing.

This little phrase "doing your own thing" originated with the rebellious hippie movement of the '60s. Many of these who wanted to do their "own thing" were soon found in jails and hospitals. Some ended up lying there much like a shriveled vegetable as a result of drugs. Smoking pot was considered the "in" thing by these young rebels. Many went on to stronger drugs. Addiction became a way of life for many of them.

A great number of these kids were from well-to-do families in plush neighborhoods. Remarkable it was, that they would leave a comfortable bed in a private room full of fine clothes, gadgets, and luxuries to sleep with some flea-bitten companions in a dirty, rat-infested loft somewhere just so they could "do their own thing!"

You still see some leftovers from this. Long-haired boys following the rock music scene—sallow, pale, unhappy, pretending to be having a good time. Girls who could have enjoyed the good things of life dressing in dirty, scroungy trousers and sweat shirts, their hair looking like a hurricane warning, and many of them getting into serious moral troubles that would leave them scarred for life—just so they could have their own way and "do their own thing!"

Human nature has always been in rebellion against God. The music and dances of each generation mirror this antagonism against God, against decency, and against what is right. These people shut themselves out from the wonderful will of God, for God does have a perfect plan for each individual life.

When Jonah defied God and bought a ticket to Tarshish, fleeing from the presence of God, he was "doing his own thing" by running away from the will of God for his life—which was to preach to the people of Nineveh. He ended up in "whale's belly chapel" taking an underwater trip in the interior of a gigantic sea monster! You, too, can get into a "whale" of a lot of trouble if you ignore or bypass the will of God for your life. Jonah probably never looked, felt, nor smelled the same after being thrown up on the beach by the big, bellowing apartment-size whale he had lived in for three days and three nights. But he was ready to do business for God. And he was given a second chance (Jon. 3:1). Maybe you have been slow to obey God. Why not give up "your own thing" today and save yourself a whale of a lot of grief!

The Israelites in the book of Judges "doing their own thing" are so typical of miserable humanity all around us today. People who will not listen to the facts about death-dealing tobacco often smoke their way into the cancer clinics and heart disease wards of American hospitals. People who think they can outsmart God and get by with drinking beer, wine, or whiskey soon have hobnails on their liver and brain cells destroyed by king alcohol. Wise King Solomon describes those who are foolish drinkers of alcohol (Prov. 23). Statistics show that over 5,000 teens and youngsters are killed every year in the USA on the highways—most of them involving alcohol and doing "their own thing."

Let God have your life. Your own thing may be the path to disaster.

Questions

1. *Name some bad habits in our society today.*

2. *How did Jonah miss the will of God at first?*

ROMANCE AND SEXUAL TEMPTATION

26. The Romance of Ruth

God will lead you to the right girl or boy in His own good time if you will just give Him a chance. "Wait on the Lord," we are told more than once in the Bible. God wants you to be happy. He knows exactly who is best fitted for you. The book of Ruth is a good illustration of this.

Ruth was a girl who lived in Moab, a heathen land. She married a sickly fellow who had come with his discouraged parents from Bethlehem-Judah. After her husband died, leaving her an attractive young widow, and after her father-in-law also died, she found herself facing a real decision. Her mother-in-law Naomi determined to go back to Bethlehem-Judah, having heard that the Lord had blessed His people there.

Ruth decided to go with Naomi, even though her sister-in-law went back into the pagan life of Moab and though her mother-in-law tried to discourage her from leaving Moab, saying, ". . . it grieveth me much for your sakes that the hand of the Lord is gone out against me" (Ruth 1:13).

Ruth made the now-famous announcement to Naomi, "Entreat me not to leave thee, or to return from following after thee: for whither thou goest, I will go; and where thou lodgest, I will lodge: thy people shall be my people, and thy God my God" (Ruth 1:16).

Ruth knew there was something about Naomi and her God that she needed, too. She went with her even though it was seemingly to a life of loneliness and poverty. But you never make a mistake when you obey the will of God.

In those days farmers left the gleanings of their crops in the field for the poor people to obtain grain just by picking it up (gleaning).

Ruth went out in the fields to glean the leftover grain for food for her and Naomi. In the providence of God she ended up in the field of a wealthy landowner named Boaz. He was a kinsman of Naomi and a very kind man who knew the Lord. He was a good man to work for.

When Boaz saw Ruth, his heart skipped a beat. "Who is this pretty and winsome girl out there gleaning in the fields?" he asked. He soon found out that she was from Moab and that she had come back to Israel with Naomi. Boaz introduced himself and told her to keep on gleaning in his field, even urging her not to go to the field of another. He had to see more of her and find out more about this Ruth!

You see, if you behave and wait on God, He will send the right person along in His own good time. Boaz fell for Ruth. He commanded the young men who worked for him to keep their hands off this girl from Moab and to see that she was refreshed with water and food when she needed it. This was unusual for a landowner to take so much interest in the poor people who came to glean in his fields.

Just as Ruth waited on God and God caused Boaz to take an interest in her, so Boaz was surprised to find this lovely and beautiful girl in his own fields, right under his nose, so to speak. But he was a godly man and should not have been surprised. God has many delightful things in store for those who wait upon Him. So just live for God and let *Him* supply the right one!

Boaz told his field workers to allow some of the grain to fall by handfuls right in front of Ruth, as if by accident. But of course, it was done on purpose. This is just like our heavenly Boaz, the Lord Jesus; He often lets handfuls of blessing fall on purpose for His own obedient children. "No good thing will he withhold from them that walk uprightly" (Ps. 84:11).

Ruth took her time. She didn't rush Boaz. And he didn't get too hasty in pursuing her.

Ruth lying at the feet of Boaz is not to be misunderstood. There is nothing dirty or suggestive in this. Customs were strange in those days. But she was a virtuous woman, as Boaz admitted. She had done no wrong. And he was most anxious that no one think evil of her or imagine that any kind of immoral activity was going on. He was, indeed, a kinsman of Naomi and the family. Be careful not to read anything into this that is not there.

He continued to load her down with gifts (Ruth 3:15–17). This is always pretty good proof that a man has been smitten by "the love bug."

In the last chapter the romance is consummated by a lovely wedding, and they lived happily ever after. Ruth married a very wealthy and wonderful husband—just by waiting on and obeying the Lord, and by having proper respect for Him and for the mother-in-law, Naomi, with whom she lived.

Soon a little baby came into their home. From that union ultimately came David the king, and later David's greater Son, the Lord Jesus! What a romance!

Questions

1. Though Ruth had been brought up in pagan Moab, she had seen so much of God in Naomi that after the death of her husband she determined to do what?

2. How did her willingness to work in the fields pay off?

3. Why do you suppose Boaz did not want her to glean in any other field?

27. So Help Me, Hannah

God has put it naturally into the heart of a woman to want to be the mother of a child. Hannah was no exception. Hannah was a favored and lovely young bride, but her womb had been shut up so that she could not bear children (1 Sam. 1:5–6). This was a great sorrow to her heart. Others provoked her and accused her because she was unable to have a child.

But God is a God of miracles. He was the One Who had for some reason shut up her womb, and He was certainly able to cure the situation. Hannah prayed earnestly that God would give her a child. Her husband went in to her and the Lord remembered Hannah and she conceived (1 Sam. 1:19).

Hannah "bare a son" and called his name Samuel, meaning "heard of God."

As a pastor I heard many couples say that they were unable to have children. But doctors do not always know and count on our mighty God. After much prayer and waiting on God, many of these couples have had a baby born into their home, after all.

Hannah had help from the Lord. She was a true and devoted young mother and refused to make a trip until her child had been weaned. In other words, her baby was breast-fed, and she faithfully stayed with him to watch her child grow up to be healthy and happy (1 Sam. 1:21–23).

Hannah declared that Samuel would be "lent" to the Lord as long as he lived. He was her boy, but she knew God had sent him to her. She gladly gave him back to the Lord. Samuel became a great man of God, one of Israel's finest prophets.

Sometimes very fine Christian couples find that for some physical reason they cannot bear children. In that case, they need to earnestly seek the Lord, as Hannah did, to get help from the Lord. Hannah had prayed earnestly for some time. If, after much prayer, God does not send a child, then Christian couples can seek wisdom from God about adopting children.

One of the terrible things about abortion is not only the killing of an unborn child in the womb, but there are so many good couples waiting and praying for a child. How much better it would be if people who do not want their expected baby would allow some family to adopt the child rather than to forever live with the tormenting knowledge that they had snuffed out a little life.

Questions

1. *Why do most normal women want to be the mother of a child?*

2. *What does this story teach us about prayer?*

3. *Give one or more reasons why abortion is wrong.*

28. Fornication—the Boys Who Made Themselves Vile

Fornication (the sex act outside of marriage) is another word for adultery; it is the same immoral act, though adultery is the word used when the scarlet sin involves a married person who "steps out" on his or her mate.

Fornication is not to be even once mentioned among the saints of God. For what people talk about, they think about, and what they think about, they are more easily tempted to do. In other words, no Christian should ever get involved in sex lust or sexual involvement before marriage, and it should not even be discussed. The sons of Eli were so evil that they committed acts of immorality with women who came to bring their sacrifices to the Lord "at the door of the tabernacle of the congregation" (1 Sam. 2:22).

These young men refused to hear the warnings and admonition of their father, Eli, and went right on with their wickedness. When young people disobey their parents, there will always be trouble. Of course, Eli was not a very strong dad. God rebuked him because "his sons made themselves vile, and he restrained them not" (1 Sam. 3:13). Because Eli had not been a good disciplinarian and had not made his boys obey, his house was to suffer judgment forever.

Soon the two young fornicators were killed in battle. The news of their death so shocked their elderly father that he fell and broke his neck and died (1 Sam. 4:14–22). The whole land of Israel suffered because of the sins of these young men.

Fathers are to make their boys obey as Abraham did. God said, regarding Abraham, "I know him that he will command his children . . . after him" (Gen. 18:19). Eli failed to do this. You need to thank God if you have parents who make you obey and who teach you what is right and what is wrong.

Fornication is not to be once named (or considered) among God's children. It is filthy and along with it goes other kinds of filthiness (Eph. 5:3–5). People who look at that which is filthy, tell dirty jokes, or listen to filthy music will soon *be* filthy and will be engaged in the terrible sin of fornication.

"No whoremonger nor unclean person has any inheritance in the kingdom of heaven." People who do such things testify that they are in darkness, but Christians are the children of light. We are not to have fellowship with the unfruitful works of darkness, and it is a shame to even speak of the things that are done by such people (Eph. 5:5–12). There are some things that we should not even discuss with others. It is a shame that preachers and parents sometimes have to mention such things to warn their children, but God is not pleased with the wicked things that sinners do and say—He does not want us talking like they talk and acting like they act.

Fornication is one of the things that brings the wrath of God upon the children of disobedience (Col. 3:5, 6).

God reminds us that 23,000 people died in one day (1 Cor. 10:8), because some people in the Old Testament committed fornication. That's what God thinks about premarital sex or sexual indulgence, with anyone except one's own marriage partner.

There were terrible things that took place in Sodom and Gomorrah. The cities were given over to fornication and "going after strange flesh" (homosexual vice). They were "filthy dreamers." They had fantasies about strange and weird sexual behavior; they defiled the flesh; they despised dominion and spoke evil of any dignitary (preacher, teacher, parent, judge) who warned them of their evil ways (Jude 7, 8). Because of this, God wiped out that whole population of sinners when fire fell on those cities (Gen. 19).

There is a day yet future when God will bring terrible plagues of judgment upon a Christ-hating, sin-loving world, but they will refuse to repent of their sorceries (witchcraft, drugs, vile music), their fornication, and their thefts (Rev.

9:21). Don't live so that you will have to suffer such judgment.

"Flee fornication" (1 Cor. 6:18). Run from it. Stay away from such evil. Don't let sexual sin destroy you as it did the sons of Eli.

Questions

1. Why should fornication not even once be named among God's people?

2. How else could Eli have helped his boys in addition to talking to them?

3. How can looking at and listening to filthy things make one become vile?

4. Since "the body is not for fornication" (1 Cor. 6:13), how should the Christian look upon his body?

29. David and "Dear Abby"

David was a brilliant and handsome army captain. A man in such position may have more tempting women around him than he needs. The ladies lined the sidewalks as David returned from his conquests in battle, crying, "Saul hath slain his thousands, and David his ten thousands" (1 Sam. 18:7). They "fell" for David. He was a magnetic personality. This aroused the green-eyed monster of jealousy in King Saul who purposed to get rid of the popular young captain.

Saul decided to give David his daughter, Michal, in marriage, knowing that she was the kind of a woman who would "be a snare to him" (1 Sam. 18:21), and would finally play him into the hands of the brutal Philistines. Thus Saul would be rid of David.

It is certainly better to pursue your own mate and not let someone else do the matchmaking. In this case Saul had an ulterior motive, indeed.

Because of Saul's intent to kill David, David went into exile and finally had to flee from the land. Evidently King Saul took his daughter, Michal, back home to live with him, where she could no longer be a tool to destroy David.

In exile David had many mighty men with him. They were kind and protective to the shepherds of a wealthy and wicked man named Nabal. But when David and his men were hungry, the wicked Nabal would do nothing to help. Therefore David and his men got their swords and were ready to pay Nabal a visit. Four hundred strong, they were determined to get food from Nabal, for you see, there was no supermarket in the wilderness.

Some of Nabal's servants went to his beautiful, wise, and charming wife Abigail, to let her know that David's warriors were coming. Abigail decided to go meet them with an abundance of food and delightful things to appease the appetite and thirst of David's men.

Abigail intercepted David and let him know how cruel and churlish her husband was. One wonders how Nabal had ever talked this great lady into marrying him in the first place! Maybe she had inherited him, since most girls in those days did not have much to do with selecting their own husbands. How much better it is today!

Anyway, this dear Abby (Abigail) fell at the feet of David and persuaded him to let her handle Nabal and that she would see that David and his men were well rewarded for their kindness to her shepherds and other employees (1 Sam. 25:23–31).

David was very much impressed, and he had sense enough to listen to Abigail. He saw in this very beautiful Abigail the wisdom of a very kind woman and dutiful wife. This kind of wife any man would want, but Abigail was married to the wicked and brutish Nabal. What a contrast to the scheming Michal whom Saul had thrust upon David.

The proud and haughty Nabal made a big feast like that of a king. He drank himself into a stupor until his heart seemed to freeze within him, and he became like stone (paralyzed). The Lord smote Nabal and he died (1 Sam. 25:38). With Nabal dead and buried, this left Abigail free to become the bride of David, who was soon to become the new king of Israel. If you wait upon God, He will in His own way and in His own time take care of the details.

The wise David had listened to the counsel of his own "dear Abby" (Abigail), and now she was his wife.

God can take care of the problems, if we will let Him. God knows just where every good husband and wife is. As He brought Adam and Eve together in Eden, He is still anxious to establish happy and godly marriages.

Questions

1. *Why was King Saul so afraid of David?*

2. *What made Saul jealous?*

3. *Why was David willing to listen to Abigail?*

4. *What great spiritual lesson about marriage do we learn from this story?*

NO HUMAN FATHER

30. The Virgin Birth

Jesus was born of a virgin. He had no human father. Until Christ, every child since Adam and Eve had come into being by means of human procreation—that is by the union of a human father and mother. But Jesus was God the Son, the promised Savior. He always existed; He was with the Father before the world began. "God so loved the world that he gave his only begotten Son" to be our Redeemer. He was conceived of the Holy Ghost. God spoke through the prophet and said, "Behold, a virgin shall conceive, and bear a son, and shall call his name Immanuel" (Isa. 7:14), which means "God with us."

Before Joseph and Mary *came together,* she was found "with child of the Holy Ghost." Joseph was amazed and confounded that his pure, lovely young bride-to-be could be expecting a baby, and God assured him that he was not to fear to take

Mary to be his wife. She was with child because the Holy Spirit had performed this miracle of conception and that, when she brought forth her son, He was to be named JESUS "for he shall save his people from their sins" (Matt. 1:19–21).

Out of the ivory palaces of heaven, came the divine Son of God to die in our stead on the old rugged cross. This is the real meaning of the virgin birth.

"Jacob begat Joseph the husband of Mary, of whom was born Jesus, who is called Christ" (Matt. 1:16). Notice how carefully the Holy Spirit guards the truth that Joseph was not the father of Jesus; He was "the husband of Mary, **of whom was born Jesus.**" Mary was His earthly mother, but Joseph was not the earthly father of this miracle Child. And Mary was only the mother of the body Jesus lived in; there is no "mother of God."

We have the divine account of Mary and her anticipation of the birth of her Son. She was a "virgin espoused to a man whose name was Joseph" (Luke 1:17–35). The angel said to her, "thou shalt conceive in thy womb, and bring forth a son, and shalt call his name JESUS . . . the Holy Ghost shall come upon thee, and the power of the Highest shall overshadow thee: therefore **that holy thing** which shall be born of thee shall be called the Son of God."

Only of Jesus could it ever be said that One was born without a human father.

Questions

1. How was Jesus' birth different from all other births?

2. How was Jesus conceived, if there was no human father?

3. What did the name "Emmanuel" mean?

MORE BITTER THAN DEATH

31. Old Testament Soap Operas

Again and again God records the sins of Old Testament people, not to make spicy "soap opera" reading, but to show us the foul consequences of sin. Here are some of them:

An Evil Friend

When Amnon, one of the sons of David, became inflamed with lust for his own half sister (2 Sam. 13), he "had a friend" who was not really a friend after all. The friend devised a plan by which Amnon could "play sick" and get the beautiful Tamar (his half sister) to come into his bedroom and take care of him. Soon Amnon took advantage of Tamar, and she was shamed (raped) and went from the house weeping. Absalom, the dashing and flamboyant brother of Tamar, determined to get revenge. Later at a party he had Amnon killed. This broke the heart of King David, so we see the pain the king was to suffer because of his earlier "affair" with Bathsheba. The death of Amnon was said to be "by the appointment of Absalom," but it was also a part of God's appointment in His public judgment of David for his previous sin with Bathsheba.

The Concubines

Many men in those olden days had concubines—women who were around the place for the convenience of the adult family members. They did many of the family chores; some were maids and household servants. They were also sometimes used to satisfy the lust of evil masters. When Absalom wanted to humiliate his father, David, he spread a tent upon the housetop and "went in unto his father's concubines in the sight of all Israel" (2 Sam. 16:22). Of course, later Absalom was to pay dearly for his sin.

Don't ever think that adulterers get away with it. When Absalom tried to take the kingdom from his father, Absalom's long, flowing hair got caught in a tree branch, pulling Absalom off his mule, and his body was riddled with darts by his enemies (2 Sam. 18:9–14). End of that "soap opera."

King Solomon's Many Women

Solomon was a great, wise, and wealthy king. But when he was older, his heart was turned away from God because of women. God had said that His people should not go in to nor affiliate with the heathen women around them.

"But king Solomon loved many strange women" (1 Kings 11:1). After becoming so enamored of women, "Solomon did evil in the sight of the Lord, and went not fully after the Lord, as did David his father" (1 Kings 11:6). His wives soon weakened him so that he was compromising with his religion and building altars unto strange gods. Because of Solomon's "strange wives," he burnt incense and sacrificed unto their strange gods! Solomon took unto himself 700 wives and 300 concubines! And eventually his wives turned his heart away from God. Much of the great wisdom of the book of Proverbs came to us because Solomon learned many heart-felt lessons that can save us from a lot of grief, if we will only listen.

Sex lust has turned many a person away from true devotion to the Word of God and caused them to compromise with "strange gods." When a Christian begins to compromise in his Bible doctrines and beliefs, he may soon become immoral in his life. And almost always, if a man begins to practice sexual sins, he will water down the gospel message and leave out some or much of "thus saith the Lord!"

How does God feel about this? Notice: "the Lord was angry with Solomon, because his heart was turned from the Lord God of Israel" (1 Kings 11:9). So "the Lord stirred up an adversary unto Solomon." In other words, God let an enemy come in and plague Solomon because of his sins of sexual indulgence, loose living, and his turning away from the true God unto idols!

God was displeased with the Jews that entered into marriages with the heathen. The Jews had "married wives of Ashdod, of Ammon, and of Moab" (Neh. 13:23). God rebuked this practice very strongly, saying, "Did not Solomon king of Israel sin by these things? . . . God made him king over all Israel: nevertheless even him did outlandish women cause to sin." The next verse speaks of "marrying strange wives" as a "great evil." So we see that God offers a very strong warning against a believer marrying an unbeliever.

Questions

1. *Why does God record some of the stories of lust and sin in the Bible?*

2. *How did Amnon pay for his sin?*

3. Solomon was a wise king, but in what way did he act stupid?

4. What caused Solomon to worship idols and honor strange gods?

32. Painted Faces

Jezebel was the first woman we have any Scriptural record of who "painted her face" (2 Kings 9:30). I do not believe this is a Scriptural rebuke against a Christian girl using makeup to help her color or, on dress-up occasions, to make herself look nicer or more natural. Evidently Jezebel plastered it on so that she looked unnatural and gaudy. Those who practice pagan religions have been noted for painted faces. Heathen natives around pagan campfires usually streak their faces with gaudy paint. Harlots have usually been marked by the over painting of their faces. When I was a boy, these were the "floozies" or street walkers—fallen women, in other words.

The rock stars, male and female, often cover their faces with paint so that they are almost unrecognizable as human beings. Satan, of course, is back of such excesses. While there is no virtue in a Christian girl looking pale and ghostly, it is unlikely that the Lord is pleased with one of His own dear children spreading on gaudy paint until they look like an imitation of Jezebel.

All of this points back to the big mistake Ahab made in marrying a pagan wife. "Ahab . . . did evil in the sight of the Lord above all that were before him . . . He took to wife Jezebel the daughter of Ethbaal king of the Zidonians, and went and served Baal [a false god] and worshiped him." Having married the ungodly, painted, idol-worshiper Jezebel, Ahab did "more to provoke the Lord God of Israel to anger than all the kings of Israel that were before him" (1 Kings 16:30–33). Ahab was no good anymore to God or to man after he made the great mistake of marrying Jezebel. You see, God is very much concerned with whom we marry. So we had better be sure that we consult Him about it and that we never marry contrary to His Word!

Years later, kings were still reaping the evil deeds that Ahab had sown. Jehoram, another king of Judah, "walked in the way of the kings of Israel, like as did the house of Ahab: for he had the da*ughter* of Ahab to wife: and he wrought that which was evil in the eyes of the Lord" (2 Chron. 21:6).

And later when Ahaziah became king, "He also walked in the ways of the house of Ahab: for his *mother* was his counsellor to do wickedly" (2 Chron. 22:3). The mistakes we make in court-ship and marriage will cause heartache years later to those who follow in our path. The lesson is that we should marry in the Lord and inspire our children to do the same!

Jezebel was later thrown down from a high tower onto the pavement, run over by chariot wheels until she was cut in pieces, and her flesh was then devoured by dogs (2 Kings 9:33). The end of her life was like her life—violent!

Questions

1. For what gaudy and worldly fashion is Jezebel known?

2. What is probably the connection between the painted faces of native heathen dancers and the painted faces of rock stars?

3. How did Jezebel cause King Ahab to sin?

33. The Unborn Child Is Alive!

Abortion is the deliberate murder of an unborn baby while still in its mother's womb. Today many people demand their "rights" to do what they want with "their own bodies," as they put it. The courts in America have made it legal to snuff out the life of the baby before it is ever born. They justify this atrocious act by saying that it is merely a "fetus" they are destroying. But that fetus, or unborn child, is very much alive in its mother's womb.

It is a known fact that the behavior of the mother and the habits of the mother while carrying that child have a great effect upon the baby. If the mother smokes, the baby is affected by the tobacco. A drinking mother is doing great damage to her unborn child with every drink of alcohol she takes. Mothers who fight, fuss, or endure great stress give stress to the baby.

Almost every child has felt the "kick" of that little unborn baby who is soon to become brother or sister—and this before the baby is born!

Some who do not care what the Bible teaches want abortion to be legal, so they can enjoy their sins of fornication and adultery without paying the price of pregnancy. Of course, they pay a much greater price in the grief and heartache that comes from having thus disobeyed God's laws. Many times girls who have an abortion wake up crying for months or years to come and think they hear their baby crying. Every time they see a precious little baby they are made to remember their crime of abortion. There are also other physical, mental, and psychological problems that come with such disobedience.

But what does God say about this "fetus" in the womb, this living little child-to-be-born?

Job's houses were destroyed, his flocks and herds killed, his children crushed by the house falling in on them after a terrible tornado struck. Not only that, but his own wife sneered at him for his persistent faith and told him he should "curse God, and die" (Job 2:9). As Job sat in an ash heap, that was once his beautiful estate, his body covered with painful boils, he cried out in his misery, wishing that he had never been born, "Why died I not from the womb?" He states that if he had died before he was born, he would have "been at *rest*" (Job 3:11–13).

So God is here teaching that Job was very much *alive* in the womb of his mother, and he wishes that he might have stayed there and expired in his mother's womb instead of coming forth to such misery as he had recently endured. This also teaches us that little babies are "at rest" when they die. One never needs to fear that an innocent baby has perished.

Jeremiah was a great prophet of God, often called "the weeping prophet." At first he was sure that he could not speak out for God and publicly serve God. But the Lord said to him, "Before I formed thee in the belly I knew thee; and before thou camest forth out of the womb I sanctified thee, and I ordained thee a prophet unto the nations" (Jer. 1:4–5). This is a mighty blow to those who say the "fetus" inside the expectant mother is not a living child. For here we find that God formed Jeremiah in the womb, sanctified him (set him apart for service), and ordained him to be a prophet long before he was born!

David wrote, "For thou hast possessed my reins: thou hast covered me in my mother's womb . . . I am fearfully and wonderfully made: marvelous are thy works; and that my soul knoweth right well" (Ps. 139:13, 14). David acknowledges that God formed him and made him to grow even from his mother's womb. Man knows this in his soul (as David put it here, "right well"). Sinful men in their wicked minds may try to reason otherwise, but deep down in their hearts, they know they were designed and made by God's good plan. No man can make another human being. And that baby "formed in the womb!" is according to God's plan.

David says that he was "made in secret . . . and in thy book all my members were written, which in continuance were fashioned, when as yet there was none of them" (Ps. 139:15, 16). From the first, when God formed Adam, He had a plan for the creation of future beings—and that was to form them in the womb. To destroy an unborn baby, then, is to kill the plan and work of God. David said that God had been holding him up even from the time he was an unborn baby, and that it was indeed God Who had taken him out of the place of birth—from his own mother's womb (Ps. 71:6).

One of the great proofs of life in the womb is the coming of the baby Jesus—the Son of God. The angel said, "Fear not, Mary: for thou hast found favour with God. And behold, thou shalt conceive in thy womb, and bring forth a son, and shalt call his name JESUS" (Luke 1:30–31).

Mary later went down into the hill country to visit her cousin, Elisabeth, who had been told that she, too, in her old age, was to bear a child who would be John the Baptist, the forerunner and herald of Jesus. When Mary greeted her cousin Elisabeth, "the babe leaped in her womb," so you see that the baby was very much alive before he was born. The full time came for her to be delivered "and she brought forth a son."

So sex is never a play toy, and intimacy is a

very serious matter. It is never right for single people to indulge with the idea that if pregnancy occurs, we can always "destroy the fetus." That is a real child in the womb!

Questions

1. *What habits of the mother can affect her unborn child?*

2. *Why do people favor abortion?*

3. *What are some of the sad consequences of abortion?*

34. Our Secret Sins

God sees all of our sins—even the secret ones. Many sexual sins are sins that we suppose will be secret sins, but sooner or later our sins will find us out. God knows all about them. And usually sin is exposed so that everybody else knows those things that we thought would be kept "secret." "Thou has set our iniquities before thee, our secret sins in the light of thy countenance" (Ps. 90:8).

David's sin with Bathsheba had been at first a "secret sin," but soon it was a scandal and disgrace known to all. Usually this is the way it happens. Achan stole from the shambles of Jericho "in secret," but soon all Israel knew and his whole family suffered death. The woman at the well was astounded to learn that Jesus knew all about the five husbands she had had, and that He also knew that she was living with a man who was not her husband!

Your secret sins may be dirty jokes or dirty music that you listen to. You would not want your parents to know. You may have some dirty pictures hidden away. One day they will be found. Maybe it is an obscene book or magazine that you have looked at, or read by yourself, or perhaps with only one other person. Remember, our secret sins will one day be exposed "in the light of

God's countenance." There may be the temptation to watch a vulgar "R" or "X-rated" video film
with other young people. Remember those secret
sins do us much harm—and they don't remain
secret for long!

Satan will tempt you to smoke, drink, or take
drugs "in secret." But remember these things
always come out in the open sooner or later.

It might be some physical indulgence you
are tempted to "fool around with" all by yourself.
But how long do you think you can keep such
things secret? Not for long because God warns us
about secret sins.

Usually parents will help if you will allow
them to. It would be good to mention to your
parents what your temptations are; often they
can help you find ways to avoid the temptations.
It is better to discuss your temptations with your
parents instead of secretly indulging in them.
God promises a way of escape from temptation:
"There hath no temptation taken you but such as
is common to man: but God is faithful, who will
not suffer you to be tempted above that ye are
able; but will with the temptation also make a way
to escape, that ye may be able to bear it" (1 Cor.
10:13).

Questions

1. If someone wants you to engage in some secret and lustful thing, how long do you think such could be kept secret?

2. How could Jesus have known about the five husbands of the woman at the well?

35. Playing the Fool

There are those so-called friends who urge you to join them in things you know you should avoid. God knows we soon become like our companions. So God says, "My son, walk not thou in the way with them; refrain thy foot from their path" (Prov. 1:15). "A companion of fools shall be destroyed" (Prov. 13:20). Proverbs is a book of great wisdom and great warning. In the very first chapter Solomon writes, "My son, if sinners entice thee, consent thou not" (Prov. 1:10).

The second chapter is even stronger, for it not only warns us about those who would lead us into theft and violence, but it warns about perverse men and lustful women. In other words, Proverbs chapters 2 through 9 warns about sexual sin and temptation. The heart of chapter 2 is that if a young person will seek true wisdom, God will preserve the way of "his saints . . . discretion shall preserve thee, understanding shall keep thee."

We need to be delivered from the way of the "evil man" who speaks "perverse things" and who "leave the paths of uprightness, to walk in the ways of darkness" (Prov. 2:13). They "rejoice to do evil"—in other words, they get their big kicks and laughs out of evil talk and evil actions (dirty jokes, sex talk, profanity, etc.). They love "darkness . . . because their deeds are evil" (John 3:19). The places people go to drink, dance, enjoy foul jokes and adulterous entertainment, are places of darkness. Even if the lights were not so low, you couldn't see for the smoke. Some speak of making the air "blue with profanity" which is part of the darkness of evil and profane men and women.

Not only does God want a young man to be delivered from evil men but also from "the strange woman" who flatters with her words. She flirts, cusses, winks, and moves her body in such a way as to lead a young man to become excited about being with her. Sadly, there are far too many of these "strange women" around. God made a girl or a woman to be the fairest flower of His creation. There is nothing more beautiful than a lovely, modest, and virtuous young woman. She has something real and genuine about her; she does not have to flaunt her body to get attention. There is something charming about such a virtuous girl.

But the *strange* woman has forsaken the "guide of her youth" and has forgotten "the covenant of her God" (Prov. 2:17). She forsakes whatever she was taught by her mother or teachers, and she forgets the covenant of her God—the holy vows she made at one time. Thus, "her house inclineth unto death, and her paths unto the dead" (Prov. 2:18). She not only moves toward a path of destruction, but she always manages to take some gullible boy or lust-loving man along with her! We learn that men who follow this "strange woman" into her paths of sin do not "return again, neither take they hold of the paths of life." Men and women who once start playing it loose morally seldom come back to a clean and virtuous life. "The wicked shall be cut off from the earth" (Prov. 2:22). This explains many of the terrible deeds of assault, violence, and murder that we read about and see on the daily news.

David wrote, "Fools because of their transgression, and because of their iniquities, are afflicted" (Ps. 107:17). Human nature rebels at the idea that judgment comes from a holy God because of our sins. Millions of our fellow citizens today are playing the fool with sin. "Sin, when it is finished, bringeth forth death" (James 1:15).

Remember, there is no double standard with God. If it is wrong for a woman to be evil, flirtatious, and suggestive in her walk and manner, it is even more so for the man to be profane, vulgar, and adulterous. God has placed the man in the first place of responsibility. God made man first, then woman. He puts the man at the head of the home, in the pulpit of the church, and usually at the helm of governments. Men were meant to be stalwart representatives of the God

Who made them. That's one reason why so many of the warnings in the Bible are to men rather than to women. Fellows, don't play the fool!

Questions

1. *Why is the choice of our companions so important?*

2. *Why does God say some foolish men are afflicted?*

3. *When sin is "finished," what does God say comes next?*

4. *What do lost and profane men get their pleasures from?*

5. *Suggest some reasons why God puts the first responsibility on the man or boy to behave himself.*

36. Her Steps Take Hold on Hell

They are all around us today, both men and women looking for "free sex" and loose living, and many teens have been tempted to give in to such temptations. These people are "strange" because they are willing to risk reputation, health, happiness, and even their very lives for an adulterous affair. Teens break the hearts of their parents, wives forsake their husbands, and many men stupidly give up a loving, faithful wife and dear children for some "strange" woman who comes along with a "come hither" look in her eye (Prov. 5:3–5).

Congressmen have lost their prominent positions in Washington because of the "strange woman." Kings have lost their thrones for the same reason. Employees have been fired, students expelled, and murders committed because of this awful sin of fornication or adultery. Is it worth it?

"Her lips drop as an honeycomb." What she says, the way she curls her lips looks so sweet, and "her mouth is smoother than oil." Yes, she's a slick talker. But notice that "her end is bitter as wormwood, sharp as a twoedged sword," so the end of the party is ugly, bitter, and devastating.

"Her feet go down to death; her steps take hold on hell." The rock singers and Hollywood movies don't tell you about that. The Devil never gives you the whole picture.

God commands, "**Remove thy way far from her,** and **come not nigh the door of her house.**" Don't go to the house of such a person, let alone meet her out in some worldly haunt. Stay as far away as you can from evil, dirty-minded, vulgar people, whether they be male or female, who want to talk about sex and other private matters.

If you "mess around" with dirty-minded, lustful people, you will give your honor unto others (Prov. 5:9–10). Someone else will walk away with the honors you could have won, and you may wind up with no honor at all! Others will be filled with the wealth that you could have earned, and you may be working for peanuts when you could have been the president of the corporation. You may be laboring for a boss when you could have been the boss, if you had stayed straight.

"Mourning" (the weeping and remorse) is the way you will feel (Prov. 5:11) when your body is consumed with some dreadful disease like syphilis, herpes, or AIDS, and "thy flesh and thy body are consumed." Sin is just not worth it! One day you may cry, "How have I hated instruction, and my heart despised reproof; and have not obeyed the voice of my teachers [pastor, parents, teacher] nor inclined mine ear to them that instructed me!"

The rest of Proverbs 5 tells how glad you will be one day when you have been true to your God and have married a wife or a husband with whom you may enjoy the delights of married love.

God describes the "playboy" philosophy of this ungodly and twisted generation as people who are "taken" by their iniquities (sins) and tied up with the "cords" of their evil ways. "In the greatness of his folly he shall go astray." He is hogtied by sin and will die in his folly like a dumb fool.

Learn Not to Burn

"Can a man take fire in his bosom, and his clothes not be burned?" (Prov. 6:27). You know the answer to that. If you play around with fire long enough, you will get burned. Thus God wants to "keep thee from the evil woman, from the flattery of the tongue of a strange woman. Lust not after her beauty in thine heart; neither let her take thee with her eyelids" (Prov. 6:24–25). In other words, watch out for the sexy, flirtatious girl or woman who uses her God-given beauty and winks a lustful eye to try to lead you off into sin. And the girl should also watch out for that kind of boy or man.

Living a wicked life style can reduce you to poverty, and "the adulteress will hunt [like a sniper picking off victims with a rifle] for the precious life." Your life is precious, so why give it to some dirty-minded person who only wants to use you as a plaything and then cast you off to be destroyed?

No one is innocent who commits adultery. "It is good for a man not to **touch** a woman" (1 Cor. 7:1). Watch what you touch, where you touch, and who you touch! Many a terrible sin begins with a wrong touch.

The adulterer "lacketh understanding" (Prov. 6:32–33), for he "destroyeth his own soul." He (or she) will be wounded and dishonored, and his reproach shall not be wiped away. They are not able to "wipe out" or clean up the mess they have made. The sins of adultery or fornication lead to many terrible crimes of violence because of the jealous rages that they produce. Say "NO" to sin. This is the best sex education!

Questions

1. What does God say about the lips of this "strange woman"?

2. What could such sin have to do with success in business and wealth of an individual?

3. Why is it dangerous to "touch" that which is not rightfully yours?

4. Why is it impossible just to "wipe away" your sin and be done with it?

37. Like an Ox to the Slaughter

A young man is pictured going "as an ox . . . to the slaughter" when he is led off into the sin of immorality (Prov. 7:22). Proverbs chapter 7 deals with the seduction of a young man by an evil and adulterous woman; it tells what most novels and movies will never tell you—the truth about the consequences of such sin!

"My son [or daughter], keep my words, and lay up my commandments with thee." You'll be smart to know your Bible, memorize much of it, let it dwell in your heart, and use it as a defense and an armor against evil temptation. Otherwise, sooner or later, sin will overtake you as it does the young man in Proverbs 7.

Harlotry takes many forms. It does not have to be a professional harlot. It may be a miserable, unhappy wife or one who is looking for some excitement while her husband (or wife) is away. It may be a young person adventuring into forbidden territory for "kicks," so boasting can be done about such conquests. Too many boys think it is "macho" to have ruined some young girl.

God wants to "keep thee from the strange woman" who flatters with her words. Note that this boy in the street was "among the simple ones." No matter how intelligent he may have been in school, he was stupid when it came to temptation. He evidently knew who she was, while he was "cruising" around looking for temptation. He was getting a thrill out of the temptation. Notice it was a "black and dark night"; much evil is hatched under the cover of darkness.

He finally sees her, this married woman looking for cheap thrills, who, if she lived today, had probably been watching shabby soap operas on TV or reading some kind of racy confessions magazine.

Though he was not kin to her and perhaps a total stranger to her, she "kissed him" with an "impudent face." She describes her love nest, assures him that her husband will not be back for a long time, and leads him into trouble. She invites him to "take our fill of love," but these kind of people are not really talking about true love, only animal lust. "With her much fair speech she caused him to yield, with the flattering of her lips she forced him."

"He goeth after her straightway, as an ox goeth to the slaughter, or as a fool to the correction of the stocks."

That is the picture we see as this gullible young man is led as a sheep to the slaughterhouse of his own destruction. I once visited a slaughterhouse in Sioux City and saw the pathway that the unsuspecting animals take out of the pens and across the road into the slaughterhouse where they were killed and butchered.

So God commands, "go not astray in her paths. For she hath cast down many wounded" and "many strong men have been slain by her. Her house is the way to hell, going down to the chambers of death."

No matter how strong you think you are, you can be done in by the sin of illicit sex.

Questions

1. *Why was the boy in this story a simpleton?*

2. *Why is the end of such an episode called "the chambers of death"?*

SEX AFFECTS BODY, MIND, AND HEART

38. Health and Happiness

"I shall yet praise him, who is the health of my countenance, and my God" (Ps. 43:5).

Young people can become downcast, depressed, and disquieted, but God can be "the health" of our countenance, as David exclaims. God is interested in our bodies and our health.

Our feelings, distresses, and moods are often brought on by physical reasons. Sometimes we feel far away from God when in reality our digestion is bad. Perhaps we've stuffed ourselves on pizza, french fries, or milkshakes, until our bodies cry out for something a little more health-giving!

The beloved apostle John said, "I wish above all things that thou mayest prosper and be in health, even as thy soul prospereth" (3 John 2). So God wants our bodies as well as our souls to be right. God wants us in good health. Many times people suffer in their twenties and thirties (and older) because they were careless about good eating habits and other good health matters in their teens.

You are fortunate to have parents who teach you to eat vegetables and salads, whether you always want them or not. Your body is a very delicate machine and needs proper care and maintenance. Enough sleep, the right kind of food, bodily cleanliness—these are all important. And, of course, plenty of the right kind of exercise to keep your body trim and healthy.

David could not have run up that mountain toward Goliath, if he had not been in good health. Samson was no pitiful 98-pound weakling when he tore the jaws of a lion apart or waded into a thousand of the Lord's enemies with the "jawbone of an ass" (Judg. 15:15). Later, after Samson had indulged in fleshly enticements, he was weak and found that "the Lord was departed from him" (Judg. 16:20).

Solomon told us that if a young man goes after a loose, immoral girl and gets involved with her, it will be like an ox going to the slaughter and that a dart will "strike through his liver" (Prov. 7:22, 23). How did Solomon know a thousand years before Christ that if a person fooled around with alcohol and "sowed his wild oats" that it would adversely affect his liver? Medical science has only discovered that in recent decades. Many a person has a bad liver because of indulgence in alcohol.

Our bodies are the "temple of the Holy Ghost" (1 Cor. 6:19). We are to present our bodies to Him as a living sacrifice (Rom. 12:1).

You can be sure that you will be healthier and happier as a young person if you keep yourself pure and stay away from lustful and dirty situations. And you will be much happier when you come to the marriage altar *pure* and know that AIDS, herpes, or some venereal disease will never catch up with you because you have been pure in your youth.

Questions

1. *Suggest some ways we should take care of our bodies.*

2. *Why will married life be safer if you behave in your youth?*

39. Where to Keep Your Heart

When people are in love, their hearts beat faster, or so it seems. Many romantic love songs speak of the heart. Love poems have been written about the throb of the heart. Love stories abound about the young man who captures "the heart" of a fair young maiden.

God wants us someday to be in love, but most of all He urges us to know His Word and keep His sayings "in the midst of thine heart" (Prov. 4:20–21). If we first know and love the Lord, our romances and marriages will be far happier and more real and lasting. So we are to "keep thy heart with all diligence; for out of it are the issues of life" (Prov. 4:23).

After mentioning the heart, God proceeds to speak of the mouth, the lips, the eyes, the feet, and the hands (Prov. 4:24–27). The heart of man in Scripture is the inner man, the seat of his emotions and affections, and not just the physical muscle that keeps the blood circulating. What we do with our heart affects all of our being. If my heart is right, then what I do with my eyes, my hands, and my feet will be right. "Let thine eyes look right on, and let thine eyelids look straight before thee."

If my heart is in the right place, my feet will not take me into places that would dishonor the Lord. God says, "Ponder the path of thy feet." How important it is, then, that we keep our hearts with all diligence. The heart and the mind are, of course, closely interrelated. "Let this mind be in you, which was also in Christ Jesus" (Phil. 2:5).

"Thou wilt keep him in perfect peace, whose mind is stayed on thee" (Isa. 26:3). "Set your affection on things above, not on things on the earth" (Col. 3:2). Here the "mind" and the "affections" would mean what Solomon is talking about in Proverbs when he speaks of "keeping the heart with all diligence."

"Blessed are the pure in heart" (Matt. 5:8).

"As he thinketh in his heart, so is he" (Prov. 23:7).

"It is a good thing that the heart be established" (Heb. 13:9).

Your heart can deceive you, for "the heart is deceitful above all things, and desperately wicked" (Jer. 17:9). So don't be swept off your feet by some smooth-talking somebody.

Your heart can play tricks on you. You can think you are in love with someone when it is really fascination or infatuation. Or you can be "in love with love," as most of us have been, at one time or another. That just means that the person just wants to be in love very much. Some will say, "My heart told me I should marry her," and it was not the Lord's will at all, or "I felt in my heart that it was all right to let him kiss me," when really it was not right. That's why many who say they are madly in love go to the marriage altar only to be getting a divorce while carrying "a broken heart!"

So keep your heart in tune with God. Peter said, "Sanctify the Lord God in your hearts" (1 Pet. 3:15). That is, set the Lord up in your heart as your God and guide, and your deceitful heart will not constantly lead you into "heart-ache" and disappointment.

Questions

1. *Why is it not possible to always "trust your heart"?*

2. *What does it mean to be "in love with love"?*

40. The Eyes Have It!

Does it matter what we do with our eyes? We find that Job "made a covenant with" his eyes (Job 31:1). "Why then should I think upon a maid?" he inquires. In other words, Job realized that he has no business looking at and thinking about enjoying sex with "a maid." "Is not destruction to the wicked?" he continues. He goes on to realize that God sees his ways and counts all his steps. When you are tempted to want to look on someone with lust in your heart and thus desire to commit fornication or adultery, you need to remember God sees all your ways!

The big trouble with "looking upon" a woman other than one's own wife is that so often the heart walks after the eyes (Job 31:7)! Man sees, then lusts, then falls into sin. When Eve saw the forbidden fruit, she then desired and took of it. When David saw Bathsheba bathing, he lusted after her and then took her.

Our eyes can get us into trouble. A married man should only look upon, touch, and desire his own wife. A married woman should do the same. Looking on another with desire may lead to lust, and lust when it is finished "bringeth forth sin" (James 1:15).

God says we should have an eye single to the will of God. Jesus said it this way, "The light of the body is the eye: if therefore thine eye be single, thy whole body shall be full of light. But if thine eye be evil, thy whole body shall be full of darkness. If therefore the light that is in thee be darkness, how great is that darkness!" (Matt. 6:22, 23).

"Sin, when it is finished, bringeth forth death" (James 1:15).

Solomon, the wise king, said, "Let thine eyes look right on, and let thine eyelids look straight before thee" (Prov. 4:25). Watch out for wandering eyes! He goes on to say, "Ponder the path of thy feet," and then wraps it up this way: "Turn not to the right hand nor to the left: remove thy foot from evil" (Prov. 4:27). So your eyes may dictate lust to your heart, and your heart may move your feet into the direction of sin. So watch what you look upon—whether TV, magazines, posters, or books! Certainly no Christian who wants to honor God will go into the public movie house. Not only do we thus identify with the world and support an evil industry, but most of the movies shown in these days of permissiveness are dirty, profane, and immoral, which is certainly far removed from Biblical morality. No wonder so many young people are in trouble and so many marriages break up! No wonder so many professing Christians never serve the Lord effectively!

Peter speaks of evil religious folk (especially false teachers) in the last days, "Having eyes full of adultery, and that cannot cease from sin; beguiling unstable souls: an heart they have exercised with covetous practices; cursed children: Which have forsaken the right way" (2 Pet. 2:14, 15).

God especially rebukes and warns us about the false religious leader (preacher, priest, TV evangelist, etc.) who tries to preach liberty to his flock while he is full of evil himself. "While they promise them liberty, they themselves are the servants of corruption: for of whom a man is overcome, of the same is he brought in bondage" (2 Pet. 2:19). Many modern preachers and youth leaders do not preach against sin because they love their own worldly practices. They often criticize those who do preach the truth and call them "legalists!" Watch out for that!

Jesus knew what He was talking about when He said, "whosoever looketh on a woman to lust after her hath committed adultery with her already in his heart. And if thy right eye offend thee, pluck it out, and cast it from thee: for it is profitable for thee that one of thy members should perish, and not that thy whole body should be cast into hell" (Matt. 5:28, 29). Yes, the eyes have it!

This does not mean that it is wrong for a young man to enjoy the looks of an attractive girl, or that it is evil for a girl to admire a handsome man. God made them attractive, and He gave us eyes to appreciate beauty. But to look and *lust* is another thing. We need to be careful that our eyes never lead us astray.

Questions

1. *Give Bible instances of where the eyes led one astray.*

2. *Why should preachers preach against sin?*

3. *What did Jesus say about a man who looks with lust on a woman?*

41. Sex and Television

"I will set no wicked thing before mine eyes" (Ps. 101:3). Our eyes can betray us if we are not careful. Bringing pictures out of the air (and even from distant satellites in the sky) and right into our living rooms is indeed astounding, to say the least. Though TV is an amazing and wonderful invention, yet it can also be a very devious and dangerous play toy.

In many a home and in many a heart, television is a problem and a sore temptation. It is easy just to get sacked down before the tube, lazily throw our minds into neutral, and watch just any and everything, if we are not very careful.

Statistics tell us about the many murders and violent crimes that a child watches during his lifetime, if he has unbridled use of the TV set. Parents and educators remind us what a time waster TV is and how much better grades most students would make if they were not addicted to TV. Pastors and teachers talk about the evil influence of television. It is one of the great curses to the cause of Jesus Christ today, and it is one of the main reasons why so few churches have real spiritual revival.

A few Christian families feel it is such a menace that they will not have a TV set in their home; they are to be commended. Others say they carefully control what is watched or how much time is spent with the TV set. But probably very few people put the proper control on the set that they should. Most believe that it is a monster in the home, but they are willing to endure it. Others like it so much that they are willing to wreck their spiritual lives and destroy their family altars.

If your parents do not have a TV set in your home, then thank God for it and cooperate with them happily. Give your time to reading good books and enjoying other wholesome activities. If there is a TV set in your home, why not encourage the other members of the family to very carefully manage it so that it does not waste your time, destroy your spiritual life, and ruin your morals.

Keeping up with the news as it is happening, watching the Olympic games, seeing the great disasters as they happen, the newsworthy political events, the election of the President, and travel films that show things all over the world—all of these can be educational and interesting. By means of TV we can take trips to exotic jungles, to frozen arctic wastelands, to magnificent mountains, and the most picturesque waterways of the world. We can see cities by means of TV that we will never be able to travel to otherwise.

We can see nature films and enjoy fine musical programs that we could not possibly have ever witnessed without TV. So it is not all bad.

Those who enjoy sports can get right into the huddle with their favorite team and then watch the instant replay of the winning touchdown, which they could never have done if sitting in the grandstand. (It is wise to turn off the beer commercials and other offensive advertising.)

What about sex on TV? People must acquire the tobacco habit or cultivate a taste for beer or wine, for these habits do not come naturally. Even violence is not in the makeup of most of us by nature. Yet sex, on the other hand, is a God-given desire and quite naturally most people are awakened in their sexual interests by what they see.

Sex in the movies and in commercials is brazen and daring. It is so sad that many young people get their idea of what love and sex is from what they see on the TV screen! "Making love" used to mean looking at a girl with eyes full of warm admiration and perhaps enjoying ice cream or a coke together. At best, it was holding hands in a stroll down by the lake, or maybe in a moment of great desire putting one's arm around his sweetheart for a brief kiss. Love is sacred and sweet and wonderful. It should be clean and chaste and tender. Real love will best wait until marriage for intimacy.

Television gives a warped and twisted picture of love, talking about "love" when there is no real relationship at all, it only means going to bed together. And, worst of all, they appear to assume that everyone indulges in sexual embraces and fulfillment, whether they are married or not. You would never know from television that there are many millions of people who choose not to wallow around in fornication or adultery. Most television writers, by their own admission, never go to church. Probably none of them go to Bible-believing, Christ-honoring churches.

Since premarital sex is wrong, it is also wrong for young people to be slobbering over one another and caressing one another just to have something to do on a date. Television gives the wrong signals about sex, and the results are often disastrous! Television teaches the exact opposite of what God teaches about love and sex.

The bedroom scenes, the dancing, the lewd embraces and deep kisses, the scanty and sexy dress (or undress) are all evil and are of the unsaved world with its bent toward evil and corruption. God says, "Love not the world, neither the things that are in the world" (1 John 2:15) and "abstain from fleshly lusts, which war against the soul" (1 Pet. 2:11).

"Touch not the unclean thing" (2 Cor. 6:17).

"Abhor that which is evil" (Rom. 12:9).

"Let this mind be in you, which was also in Christ Jesus" (Phil. 2:5).

"Grieve not the holy Spirit of God" (Eph. 4:30).

"Set your affection on things above" (Col. 3:1).

"Whatsoever ye do in word or deed, do all in the name of the Lord Jesus" (Col. 3:17).

All of this should be enough to let us know that the *sex* of television is not the pure kind of love between husband and wife that God speaks of in His precious Word!

Questions

1. *Why is the temptation for sex different than that of tobacco, drink, or drugs?*

2. *Describe the religious life of the scriptwriters for movies and television programs.*

3. *How does TV give a warped view of love?*

42. Alcohol and Sex

It has been said that the sex powers bring with them certain temptations, but they also bring a challenge to self-mastery that should ring like a bugle call to every red-blooded man and woman in the land, but that bugle call is muted when alcohol enters the scene.

"Thine eyes shall behold strange women," describes the man whose senses are blurred by alcohol (Prov. 23:29–33). The "strange women" (evil women of sensual pleasure) always show up in the presence of beer, wine, and whiskey.

After describing the lewd, sultry, and strange woman who lies "in wait" to take her "prey," "and increaseth the transgressors among men," a very vivid description of the drinking man is given; he has "woe . . . sorrow . . . contentions . . . babbling . . . wounds without cause . . . redness of eyes"! That is a picture of the typical drunk. He has woe and sorrows he'd never have without his drinking. He (she) gets into fights or "contentions" that are usually brought on by beer or cocktails. He babbles and talks with a thick, idiotic tone to his voice, often rattling on for hours with nothing to say. He often ends up with "wounds without cause," bruises and cuts from his stumbling and staggering. His eyes are red and bloodshot. His thinking processes are marred. He goes after the "strange woman." The next day someone may sue him or blackmail him.

He is among those who "tarry long at the wine," not realizing that "at the last it biteth like a serpent, and stingeth like an adder."

Note the sex connection to his drinking: "Thine eyes shall behold strange women." He finds himself making over (or pawing over) women who are strange to him; it could be somebody else's wife, a professional prostitute, or a family member (incest). He probably wouldn't give them a second look, if he were sober. If this strange woman is another drunk's wife, he may end up in a barroom fight. This is the cause of many brawls and murders that hit the front pages of our newspapers. His "wounds without cause" would not have happened if he had been sober (Prov. 23:29).

"Thine heart shall utter perverse things." The drinking man (or youth) will say evil and vulgar things he might never say if he had not been drinking.

Many times the drunkard gets so tipsy that he'll stagger around like one trying to lie down in the midst of the waves of the sea, or like someone asleep on the top of a ship's mast. He denies he is drunk. He can be beaten or hurt but doesn't notice it, because his senses are dulled. When he wakes from his stupor, he seeks the bottle again! He is addicted to his own ruin. And one of the by-products of his drinking is sexual misconduct.

The prophet Isaiah speaks of those who have become "inflamed" by wine (Isa. 5:11–12, 22). Many people today are so inflamed. Isaiah tells how the glorious God-given beauty of a person can become a "fading flower" because of alcohol (Isa. 28:1, 3). Proud drunkards, the prophet says, can be easily trodden under foot; that is, walked over by others because all their manhood has been drained away by their drinking.

Isaiah 28:7–8 describes how people err and go "out of the way" through drink. They get on the wrong road, for sure. He says that even the prophet and priest can so destroy themselves. Unsaved preachers and priests (and there are many of them) often take to the bottle (sexual impurity usually goes with it) because they have not the true Spirit of God within them to give them victory. Drinking and the indulgences that go with it often lead to "tables full of vomit and filthiness."

Habakkuk 2:15 puts strong drink and nakedness together, so again we see that those who drink are much more likely to fall into sexual vice and ruin. Dirty dancing and lewdness will be found almost always where people go to drink alcoholic beverages. If you want to flee sexual temptation, then avoid beer, wine, or liquor as you would a terrible plague!

Questions

1. Why do evil women hang around beer and alcohol haunts?

2. What are some of the ways Solomon describes the drunkard that is so appropriate today?

3. Why does the drinker say perverse things and commit deeds he can't remember?

43. Sex and Idolatry

Adultery (sex looseness) and idolatry are usually connected in the Bible. "Will ye steal, murder, and **commit adultery,** and swear falsely, and **burn incense unto Baal,** and **walk after other gods** whom ye know not?" (Jer. 7:9). Those involved in adultery and other vices were also going after idols—false gods, like Baal.

God links sexual defilement with lifting up one's eyes to idols (Ezek. 18:6). The sins of Jerusalem are revealed as harlotry, for God traces their physical growth from babyhood to maturity, comparing their idol worship and images to their excursions into sex-lust and impurity (Ezek. 16). Sex and idolatry often go together.

This makes it easy to understand why those in false cults usually have little or no morals. Some actually indulge in sexual vice as part of their worship. Of course, such religious idolatry is of the Devil, who well knows the weakness of the flesh; thus Satan has a field day in destroying people.

Jim Jones, a recent cultist of renown, led his followers to give up their families and all ties to America and follow him to Guyana, South America, where he brainwashed his followers into practicing perversion, homosexuality, and adulteries as a part of their worship. After Satan had defiled them and duped them, the next step was to follow their idolatrous leader to death. Over 900 of them perished either by taking poison or were murdered for refusing to do so. And all of this in the name of religion!

It is easy to see how a holy God frowns upon physical adultery and the spiritual adultery of idol worship.

Ezekiel 22 shows the sex connection to idolatry: they commit lewdness, are naked, and commit sexual abomination even with their own family members. They are also involved in bloodshed and extortion. Sin is progressive.

Daniel is the classic example of a young man (believed to be still in his teens) who "purposed in his heart that he would not defile himself." Daniel's name means "God is my judge." He descended from Judah and was probably of royal blood. As Christians *we* are children of God, royal blood indeed, and God will be our judge also. Daniel knew that the fear of the Lord is the beginning of wisdom. He had backbone as well as breeding and manners, so he made God's honor roll. He refused the idolatry of his day.

He would rather go to the lion's den than to give in and deny his God by refusing to pray (Dan. 6). So he came out of the lion's den unharmed, unscathed, and undefiled. Whatever the Devil was for, Daniel was against. That is the way it ought to be for us today.

The Bible teaches sexual purity. One way to stay pure is to avoid all idolatry—religious and otherwise.

Questions

1. *Idol worship and impurity frequently went together in Bible times. How does it compare to the world today?*

2. *Daniel stayed pure by purposing what?*

44. Evolution, Sex, and Atheism

A caretaker ranger at Yellowstone National Park was viewing the gorgeous winter scenes—the snow covered mountains, ice-dripping waterfalls, and all of the frozen splendor—and said that the dawning of morning there in Yellowstone and the approaching spring was "like it must have been right after creation." An honest man who views such grandeur must believe in creation. And if there was a time when everything was created, then there must be a Creator.

"The invisible things of him from the creation of the world are clearly seen (as the Yellowstone Park ranger stated), being understood by the things that are made" (Rom. 1:20).

Where did evolution come from? Evolution is the idea that man evolved from some lesser form of life in a swamp or bog in the far distant past. God tells where the theory originated and where it leads to.

Children, when they are young, automatically believe in God until some infidel teacher, reprobate parent or neighbor begin to put doubts in their young minds. But if people, even young people, do not glorify God as they see Him revealed in nature and are not thankful, their imaginations become vain and their "foolish heart"

(heart of an atheist) will be darkened. "Professing themselves to be wise" they become fools (atheists) (Rom. 1:22), for "the fool hath said in his heart, 'There is no God' " (Ps. 14 and 53).

The foolish heart (heart of an atheist) "changed the glory of the uncorruptible God into an image made like to corruptible man, and to birds, and fourfooted beasts, and creeping things" (Rom. 1:23). Here is the origin of the theory of evolution with all of its weird supposings.

Notice how evolution eventually affects the life style of those who embrace it: sex lust is the natural result of evil, godless thinking. So God gives them up "to uncleanness through the lusts of their own hearts, to dishonour their own bodies between themselves" (Rom. 1:24). Since humanism is another subtle form of atheism, it is not surprising that the humanist often has loose morals, sees nothing wrong with people living together without marriage, or young people experimenting with sex before marriage, and defending pornography and vice as "natural."

God says they change "the truth of God into a lie, and worship and serve the creature more than the Creator" (Rom. 1:25). They leave God out of their thinking, and thus they think only of man—his dreams, pleasures, and achievements.

"For this cause God gave them up unto vile affections" (Rom. 1:26) so their women become "lesbians"—they "change the natural use into that which is against nature"—they become homosexual, perverted, unnatural. It is no wonder that many advocate "homosexual rights!"

The vile, sordid cesspool of men is described as burning in their lust one toward another, "men with men," and they receive "*in themselves* that recompense of their error"—that is, in their own lives and bodies they suffer frightening sexually related diseases. The "gays" are no longer gay!

Because they "did not like to retain God in their knowledge" (Rom 1:28), they are given over to "a reprobate mind." The following verses tell all the terrible things the unbelieving mind is filled with.

There is a relationship between evil theories (such as evolution) and illicit, unnatural sex.

Questions

1. *According to Romans 1 where can the evidence for God be found?*

2. *If men reject the idea of God and yet profess themselves to be wise, they become what?*

3. *When men think such godless thoughts, they are given up to what?*

YOUNG PEOPLE AND THE INTIMATE LIFE

45. Who Owns Your Body?

Who gave you your body? "What hast thou that thou didst not receive?" (1 Cor. 4:7). David reminds us that it is God Who hath made us and not we ourselves. We are His people. This is true of all men, even unbelievers; they are God's by creation. We who are saved are His both by creation and redemption.

"The body is not for fornication, but for the Lord; and the Lord for the body" (1 Cor. 6:13). In a very special way God values and delights in the bodies of His own dear children. He beseeches us to "present your bodies a living sacrifice, holy, acceptable unto God, which is your reasonable service" (Rom. 12:1).

Our bodies "are the members of Christ." Should these bodies be made "the members of an harlot? God forbid." Those who become sexually impure actually join bodies with a harlot, "for two, saith he, shall be one flesh" (1 Cor. 6:15–16). So we see what God thinks of the harlotry of fooling around with impurity.

"Flee fornication," Paul warns. If you commit this awful sin of fornication, you are sinning against this body that God has allowed you to use—a body which is really His. "Your body is the temple of the Holy Ghost which is in you, which ye have of God, and ye are not your own" (1 Cor. 6:19). We are to glorify God in our bodies and in our spirits.

"It is good for a man not to touch a woman" (1 Cor. 7:1). Isn't that extreme? Remember, that Paul wrote to the Corinthians who were known for their licentious (lacking moral restraint) living. Many of them were given over to vile passions and loose living. Thus, when a Corinthian became a Christian, he still had to battle his environment as well as his habits of life. It was awfully easy to give in to a seductive touch or caress. It would have been easy to go on "touching" and handling forbidden fruit. So Paul wrote that it is safer just not to touch someone you might get involved with.

Today we also need the warning to be careful who we touch and where we touch. If young people hold hands and snuggle up too warmly on a date, there is always the danger of yielding to temptation as the desire increases and inhibition fades. The light kiss on the cheek at the end of a date can be replaced by heavy, long, slobbery kisses like we see worldlings do on TV!

Remember our bodies belong to the Lord; therefore, we must be careful that the closeness of that person we like, and the aggressiveness of his or her hands, does not lead to petting or fondling that could kindle a fire of lust. All of us should beware of touching anyone in an affection-ate way who should be off-limits to us. Solomon warned in Prov. 6:29 that when it comes to a neighbor's wife, "Whosoever toucheth her shall not be innocent." Often, people complain of trouble they've gotten into when, in reality, it was a careless touch that brought it on. Preachers, then, need to be careful about their female members, and women in the church, including young girls, must beware of putting their hands where they do not belong. Christians are told to love one another, but this simply means Chris-tian love and esteem, never physical affection or familiarity. Men who are in Christian work should be careful of the problem of "touch." Young lady, never create a problem for your youth director or music director.

Adults, "to avoid fornication" (1 Cor. 7:2), are to have their own husbands or their own wives, and to "render unto them" the affection and love their partner needs. But in the mean-time, while you are a single young person, it is vital that you are careful not to allow some "touch" in the wrong place, for at the wrong time it may lead to trouble and possible disaster. Many a tragedy has started with a touch. Your body is sacred. It belongs to God. Keep it clean, strong, and yielded to Him for His glory.

Questions

1. *What does God say about His ownership of our bodies?*

2. *How does God picture the body?*

3. *What did God say about touching?*

4. *How can a touch cause trouble?*

46. The Bare Truth about Modesty

Is it important to be able to blush? It was said about an idolatrous people, "neither could they blush" (Jer. 8:12).

God commands, "that women adorn themselves in modest apparel . . . with shamefacedness and sobriety" (1 Tim. 2:9). Obviously it means that the girl or woman should be able to blush. This sounds strange in a generation where advertising, entertainment, and society in general accepts and even applauds women and girls in shorts, miniskirts, and skimpy bathing suits. But this shows how far we have drifted from Biblical standards of modesty.

It was said about the wicked people of Jeremiah's day, "Were they ashamed when they had committed abomination? nay, they were not at all ashamed, neither could they blush: therefore shall they fall among them that fall . . . I will surely consume them, saith the Lord" (Jer. 8:12–13). God knows that if people begin to dress like the world in scant attire and lose their "blush," that they will soon fall and find themselves doing things God never intended. So don't ever take the matter of modesty lightly. This is one good way to stay away from sexual temptation.

When the maniac of Gadara, the man who had been raging, unclothed, and in the tombs, was converted, he was found, "sitting, and clothed, and in his right mind" (Mark 5:15). If we are in our "right mind," we will be properly clothed. Never lose your blush!

Questions

1. Are people in general today "ashamed" of their abominations?

2. Name some attire for girls that is immodest.

47. Learn to Say "Nay!"

"Say 'NO' to drugs"—a slogan coined to discourage drug abuse. The same "NO" or "Nay" is an excellent word to remember when tempted by the world's fascinating allurements in the physical and sexual realm. In the past, college presidents, professors, doctors, and scientists gave very stern warnings to young people to say "No" to sin and physical indulgence. They gave shocking warnings about venereal diseases, long before herpes and AIDS came on the scene. These were educators and medical professionals who had "horse sense" (stable thinking!).

In Jeremiah's day people gave themselves over to such indulgence: "their transgressions are many, and their backslidings are increased." God cries, "How shall I pardon thee for this? . . . they then committed adultery, and assembled themselves by troops in the harlots' houses . . . every one neighed (desired) after his neighbor's wife" (Jer. 5:7–9). When the people fell into lust, they became discontented with their own wives and husbands. "Shall I not visit for these things? saith the Lord: and shall not my soul be avenged on such a nation as this?"

To live in such sin is to deal "very treacherously" against the Lord, and they became so intrenched in their lust that they thought God would have to overlook it. They said, "neither shall evil come upon us" (Jer. 5:11–12). So today people try to refuse to believe that God will hold them accountable for their sins that lead to divorce and ruin. They refuse to accept the fact that God has sent horrible diseases as a judgment upon the vile sins of adultery, fornication, and perversion.

People who are smart today will learn from this and determine to say "Nay" to illicit sex, pornography, drugs, rock music, and anything else that leads to such vile affections and practices. Have the courage to say NO!

It is terrible, but true, that people can become like beasts if they let themselves go and follow the "bent" of their evil hearts!

Violence will continue to get worse, the Bible teaches, until Jesus returns. Young people will be wise to fortify themselves and dare to stand for purity. Today as in Jeremiah's day, "the land is full of adulterers; for because of swearing the land mourneth . . . their course is evil . . . For both prophet (preacher) and priest are profane; yea, in my house have I found their wickedness, saith the Lord" (Jer. 23:10–11). This explains religious leaders falling into sin. In some instances they are not saved preachers or priests at all. In other situations they have embraced error in doctrine and thus "water down" the Bible. Still others may be sincere Christian leaders who have not fortified themselves against temptation but have compromised and given in to the allurements of this sensual age.

The devil will do all in his power to ruin anyone who represents the Lord, and especially those who are being truly used of the Lord. So all Christians need to beware and "put on the whole armor of God."

Questions

1. Why did Jeremiah tell us that God had to bring judgment (punishment) upon the people of his day?

2. Suggest some reasons why even preachers or priests may go bad.

48. How to Stay in Control

Christian young people (as well as adults) can easily lose control in the realm of moral purity if they are not extremely careful. An auto is a fine machine as long as it is under control. Fire is good when contained, but terrible when it is out of control. Let us look at some words that tell young Christians how to morally stay in control.

Talk

Watch your words. After God's warning about fornication and uncleanness, He commands, "Neither filthiness nor foolish talking, nor jesting" (Eph. 5:4). In the context it is easy to see that the foolish talk and jesting relates to the filthiness and fornication spoken of here. Be careful what you laugh and joke about! Don't let evil companions lure you into filthy speech and dirty jokes. There are some things we are not to joke about. God puts the unclean (dirty-mouthed) person in the same category as the idolater and whoremonger. Keep your speech clean. "Have no fellowship with the unfruitful works of darkness, but rather reprove them" (Eph. 5:11). It is "a shame even to speak" of the dirty things they do in secret (Eph. 5:12). Don't get lured into dirty talk.

Mortify

We are to "mortify" such earthly things as "fornication, uncleanness, inordinate (unregulated or excessive) affection, evil concupiscence (sexy life style), and covetousness, which is idolatry" (Col. 3:5). The word "mortify" means to destroy the strength, deaden, or subdue. So we are to put these things to death in our lives. The secret is to "seek those things which are above" and to "set your affection on things above, not on things on the earth" (Col. 3). It is what has been called "the expulsive power of a new affection."

Possess

"That every one of you should know how to possess his vessel" (1 Thess. 4:4). The vessel refers to the human body. "We have this treasure (our spiritual life) in earthen vessels" (2 Cor. 4:7). We must learn how to "possess" this vessel "in santification and honour" (1 Thess. 4:4). We are to honor our bodies by keeping them clean, covering them properly, and behaving decently. As Paul put it, "keep under my body" or keep it under proper control, "and bring it into subjection" (1 Cor. 9:27). Don't be ruled by your body and fleshly desires!

Abstain

"Abstain from fornication" (1 Thess. 4:3), and "Abstain from all *appearance* of evil" (1 Thess. 5:22). We are not only to stay out of sin but to so live that we would never give the appearance of it! We are to thus keep our testimony bright as we walk the pilgrim pathway. The movie you might go to see may be cleaner than most, but what appearance have you given in coming out of the movie theater? You may simply be identified (by your appearance) as supporting and endorsing the filthy movies of Hollywood.

You might just order orange juice or a Pepsi at the bar, but if it is an alcoholic bar, who knows what you were drinking? Watch your appearance! You might attend the high school prom and not dance, but what appearance have you given to those who see you in such a place with the smoke, the vulgar talk, and dirty music? You might not really be trying to entice or lure some man on the beach, but be careful that your appearance does not give a false signal. Stay in control.

Questions

1. How do some people let their talk get out of control?

2. Where does God say we should set our affection?

3. Why is it important to abstain even from the appearance of evil?

49. What Are You Thinking About?

God knows our thoughts. We must guard our thoughts if we would remain sexually pure. What do you think about when your mind is in neutral?

If a person truly repents of sin, that person will have to forsake evil thoughts to receive God's blessing every day.

Most sexual wrong-doing starts first in the mind or in the thoughts. The thought life is where the trouble usually starts. "As he thinketh in his heart, so is he" (Prov. 23:7). "Whatsoever things are . . . pure, think on these things" (Phil. 4:8). "Out of the heart of men, proceed evil thoughts" (Mark 7:21).

God can help us "cast down imaginations . . . and bring into captivity every thought to the obedience of Christ" (2 Cor. 10:5). We can control our thoughts if we seek the Lord's help.

People dredge up dirty jokes and foul language from a rotten and unclean heart where putrid thoughts originate. This is one of the evils of pornography. To look upon that which is nasty and unclean soon graduates from the eyes to the mind and thoughts. If our thoughts are corrupt and evil, we soon will become utterly corrupt.

Keep your mind where it belongs. "Unto the pure all things are pure: but unto them that are defiled and unbelieving is nothing pure; but even their mind and conscience is defiled" (Titus 1:15).

We cannot always keep evil thoughts from coming to mind for a brief moment. As long as we are in this world, we will see things (sometimes even by accident) that create problems in the mind and imagination. But we need not dwell on these things. "Resist the devil, and he will flee from you" (James 4:7).

"Every man is tempted, when he is drawn away of his own lust, and enticed" (James 1:14). So do not let your thoughts dwell on that which will create lust. Lust is the slimy serpent that will lead down the path of sin and death.

Read good books. Pray about all things, particularly as you begin your day. Make much of your Bible, and dwell upon its wonderful promises. Listen to wholesome and good music, and discipline those pleasure hours.

Questions

1. *Why is the thought life so important?*

2. Where did Jesus say evil thoughts originate?

3. What does pornography do to the thought life?

50. Peer Pressure in Reverse

Peer pressure is very strong for young people! Imitating everybody else, doing something wrong or adopting certain habits because other young people do, is "following the crowd." Why not be a "cut above" the crowd?

Why not set out to be an example; "Let no man despise thy youth; but be thou an example" (1 Tim. 4:12). This is peer pressure in reverse. This should be especially easy in a Christian school or church youth group. The school leaders and authorities are on your side, and the pastor, the teachers, and your parents will certainly be rooting for you. Let other young people conform to *your* mold instead of you to *theirs*. Yet, even in some Christian groups there are teens who feel they must conform to the world with its habits, fashions, music, and pleasures. Why should a Christian take delight in imitating those who are wicked and perverse? Those who imitate the world should not be surprised if people doubt that they are really saved.

"Be thou an example . . . in charity . . . in faith, in purity" (1 Tim. 4:12). We can set an example *in word*—what we say; *in manner of life*—behavior; *in charity*—our love should be pure and without hypocrisy; *in spirit*—we should be fervent in spirit, zealous, sincere, and spiritual; *in faith*—why not prove by your life that you trust God and have some real conquests in prayer to talk about; *in purity*—above all, Christian youth should purpose to stay free of sexual impurity, dirty jokes, vulgar music, rotten literature, profane language.

There will be great temptations along the way. Satan will throw the evil darts of lust at your heart. Avoid such traps. Run from evil. "Flee also youthful lusts" (2 Tim. 2:22). For "evil men and seducers shall wax worse and worse" (2 Tim. 3:13) as the coming of the Lord nears. Through dirty videos, raunchy music, evil companions, suggestive television programs, worldly fashions, etc., Satan will continue to seduce Christians if at all possible. Why not experience the thrill of turning peer pressure around and leading others to follow your example? It may take awhile. They may not follow at first. But some will, sooner or later. And the young people you influence may be the very ones God will use to shake the world!

Questions

1. *What is peer pressure?*

2. *Name some things God says we should be an example in.*

3. *Why would you think Satan would especially fling his darts at Christian young people?*

THE BRIDE AND THE BRIDEGROOM

51. Worse Than Staying Single

A recent survey, reported in a city newspaper, said that many men agreed that finding a good woman (for a wife) was a hard thing to do. However, these were worldly-wise men looking for a wife where the good ones are least likely to be found—in the bars, nightclubs, drinking parties, and other assorted haunts of sin.

God is interested in the love life of His own dear children and wants to lead them to the right mate, if indeed, they are to marry. "Whoso findeth a wife findeth a good thing, and obtaineth favour of the Lord" (Prov. 18:22). Someday you will probably be looking for a mate. The way you set your standards now will determine the type of mate you choose later.

Not to seek His will, may very well find a young man ending up with "a foolish woman" (Prov. 9:13) who is "clamorous" (loud, noisy) and is simple (dumb about truly important things); and, concerning the things that would really make her a valuable life's partner, she "knoweth nothing."

Many college-bred women and men know about calculus, computers, and constellations but may be amazingly stupid when it comes to common sense, companionship, and consideration. People can be smart about this world while knowing absolutely nothing about spiritual matters.

"I don't know anything about God," cried a pretty high school senior, who came forward to be saved, "you'll have to help me pray." The girl made good grades and was popular in school, but she knew absolutely nothing about the Bible.

Surveys reveal that young adults who are well educated and who have money and possessions are more likely to make a failure of their marriages than those from simpler backgrounds. So education is not the answer—unless that education is founded upon the Word of God.

"As a jewel of gold in a swine's snout (pig's nose), so is a fair woman which is without discretion" (Prov. 11:22). To marry a girl who has no discretion or wisdom (and remember, "the fear of the Lord is the beginning of wisdom") is the height of folly. Also, if a girl marries a spiritually ignorant man, she is asking for heartache.

Even worse is it to marry a girl who is not virtuous. "A virtuous woman is a crown to her husband: but she that maketh ashamed is as rottenness in his bones" (Prov. 12:4). Don't date or get involved with someone you'd be ashamed of in certain company, and never get serious with someone you cannot trust. Some foolish girls even marry a man who cheats on her; though she knows this while they're still single!

It would be far better to stay single.

"Fools make a mock at sin" (Prov. 14:9). Don't play the fool by marrying one! If it is dangerous (yes, disastrous) to marry a fool, it is certainly folly to date and run with one! Youth counselors say that many girls often give in to sexual proposals from their boyfriends "so they won't lose him." But what would she *lose* ?

The Bible teaches that it is a "good thing" to find a good wife, so it is surely God's plan for most people to fall in love and get married, but it is also good to know that it is a "prudent" wife God is talking about (Prov. 19:14). A prudent wife, according to the dictionary, is one marked by wisdom, one able to discipline herself, one who governs herself with skill, caution, and good judgment. The same, of course, could be said about a prudent man. Now we'll have to admit there are not too many like that today!

So the wise youth will submit to the Lord, acknowledge Him, and let Him lead them to the right mate.

"It is better to dwell in the wilderness, than with a contentious and an angry woman" (Prov. 21:19). Better to be a hermit and live in the wilds than to have the miserable company of a wife who is contentious (perverse and wearisome) and angry. One who is always argumentative and combative will soon drive the husband to the wilderness!

Of course, it is also true that a girl should look for a husband who will be kind, prudent, disciplined, and gracious. Be extremely careful during your dating days. As "a whore is a deep ditch" (Prov. 23:27), "and a strange woman is a narrow pit," so a loose, dirty-minded man will put a virtuous young wife into a state of abject misery. This is worse than staying single!

Questions

1. *Why do some men have so much trouble finding a good wife?*

2. *A fair woman, without discretion, is said to be like what?*

3. What kind of wife is a prudent one?

4. Give at least one reason why some men give up on their marriages and head for "the wilderness."

52. Not What He Bargained For

Jacob "fell" for Rachel and loved her so much that he promised her father, Laban, that he would work for him for seven years to make Rachel his bride. "Rachel was beautiful and well favored" (Gen. 29:17); in fact, when Jacob first saw Rachel he "kissed Rachel, and lifted up his voice, and wept" (Gen. 29:11). She must have been some girl!

Jacob worked seven years for Rachel "and they seemed unto him but a few days, for the love he had to her." All during those seven years he continued to love Rachel, and his work seemed like pleasure as he thought of the great joy of making Rachel his bride.

But, behold, when he took his veiled bride into his tent in the darkness of the evening, he found he had been tricked. It was not until the next morning that he realized how he had been deceived. For Laban had substituted his weak-eyed daughter Leah for beautiful Rachel, and Jacob found that he had married the wrong girl! Then he had to agree to work seven more years in order to get Rachel for his wife. Jacob had tricked his brother Esau several years before; now he was the one being tricked.

As unusual as that story is, it certainly was not the last time that a young person has married, only to realize soon that he or she did not get what they bargained for.

You'll be smart to think a long time about what kind of guy (or gal) you want to be married to. Set your standards high. Live so that you can deserve one who has great character and integrity.

Pray for God's choice in the matter. Ask Him to lead you to the right person at the right time. Then keep your eyes open during your dating days. It is awfully easy to be deceived and swept off your feet when the fires of romance begin to burn.

Questions

1. *In what way did the experience of Leah become a boomerang to Jacob?*

2. *How are some people deceived today in love matters?*

53. The Woman Who Is Priceless!

Too Young to Marry?

How young is too young to marry? Most teens are too young. Sometimes it has worked out, but there are problems. But since a man is to "rejoice with the wife of thy youth" (Prov. 5:18) and God says "I will therefore that the younger women marry, bear children, guide the house" (1 Tim. 5:14), then God evidently does not expect for you to wait until you are old! Many young people who are deeply in love (in their early twenties) might be much safer to marry and "sweat it out" about income and possessions than to keep putting it off and fall into burning temptation. God doesn't say how young is too young. Some girls are more mature at 18 than others are at 25. Wait on God! Talk to your parents and your pastor. God will lead you, if you let Him. Don't be "turned aside after Satan." And when you are married, God says the young wives should be sober; they should love their husbands and love their children. The home should be their first domain (Titus 2:4–5).

A woman whose price is "far above rubies" is known as the virtuous woman. Virtuous means a woman of virtue. If she is single, she is a virgin; she has kept herself sexually pure. But whether single or married the word *virtuous* means she is a girl or woman who is morally excellent (Prov. 31:10). This is the kind of person every girl ought to determine to be.

Another word for virtuous is "chaste." We think of a chaste woman when we think of one who is pure and virtuous. But the man should be chaste, also; he should exhibit virtue. One dictionary definition of virtue is "manly strength or courage." God wants both man and woman to be priceless!

Solomon asked, "Who can find a virtuous woman?" She may not be easy to find today, but keep looking! She's there. You don't want a wife who is one of those sleazy, sensual girls described by Solomon when he speaks of the adulterous woman, "She eateth, and wipeth her mouth, and saith, I have done no wickedness" (Prov. 30:20). In other words she has no conscience against sin. Some people practice sin, wallow in it, talk about it, dance to its tunes, until they no longer think their impurity is wickedness. Hollywood and TV promote this with regularity; they have no conscience about sin.

This virtuous, dedicated, hard-working, and faithful wife is said to excel them all (Prov. 31). No wonder "her husband is known in the gates," which means he is a well-known, responsible leader. He has been made successful partly because he had the good sense to marry this great virtuous lady. What a contrast to the "odious woman" (Prov. 30:23) whom the earth "cannot bear."

There are still girls to be found who are pure and decent. They are in good churches across the land, in Christian schools, and in some public and secular institutions. Some are clerks, salespeople, secretaries, executives, and farm girls. Remember, the more you live a virtuous life and demand decent standards, the more you will inspire others to do the same.

The heart of her husband will be able to safely trust a wife like this (Prov. 31:10–31). He knows she won't be flirting with other men, and therefore no other man can come along and spoil his happiness. "She will do him good and not evil all the days of her life." She is not afraid of hard work; "strength and honor are her clothing."

"She shall rejoice in time to come." This girl has a future!

"In her tongue is the law of kindness." She doesn't stay in a boisterous, argumentative clamor. Watch your tongue if you want to attract the right kind of mate.

"A woman that feareth the Lord, she shall be praised." This is the kind of a girl a Christian boy ought to look for.

In contrast, there is another kind of woman: "More bitter than death (is) the woman, whose heart is snares and nets, and her hands as bands: whoso pleaseth God shall escape from her" (Eccles. 7:26). God says, "Give not thy strength unto (that kind of) women" (Prov. 31:3). Many a man is drained, weak, powerless, because he has embraced this "bitter woman." Don't give your strength, time, and energy to this kind of girl. Don't play the fool, God says.

There is "a time to embrace and a time to refrain from embracing" (Eccles. 3:5). The girl or guy who always wants to display affection in public is an insecure type who is trying to prove his "conquest." If he (she) is overly zealous about touching, embracing, necking, then beware! This is not the virtuous person you want—at least they will not remain virtuous long!

Embracing, petting, and fondling has led many a person out of the "virtuous" camp into the company of the "secondhand"—greatly reduced in value. Once petting is begun, it is hard to stop; it leads many a couple into the sex act. "Because sentence against an evil work is not executed speedily, therefore the heart of the sons of men is fully set in them to do evil" (Eccles. 8:11). The wise young person will beware of such intimacy, "For God shall bring every work into judgment, with every secret thing" (Eccles. 12:14).

Behaving yourself while you are young and single will make it much easier to "Live joyfully with the wife whom thou lovest all the days of the life of thy vanity" (Eccles. 9:9). We do reap in later years what we sow in our younger years.

Questions

1. *Whose price is far above rubies?*

2. *How would you identify a chaste or virtuous person today?*

3. *The loose, immoral woman can be more bitter than what?*

4. *Why is petting and fondling dangerous?*

54. Learning to Love

"And he loved her" (Gen. 24:67). Isaac had never met the girl, but God was in it, so he loved her from the very beginning. You can learn to love, and you can choose to love.

I surrendered my life to the Lord under a pastor in Florida who is now with the Lord. He was a loving, kind, and dedicated man. His wife was a very gracious and lovely wife—one greatly loved by the people of their congregations. She made quite an impression on the young people. Theirs was a very happy marriage.

This pastor's wife insisted that she had spurned the attentions (and intentions) of this dashing young preacher and really did not feel any love for him while they were dating. She liked him very much and enjoyed his friendship but did not feel she could marry him.

He kept insisting that she was the one for him and that God had led them together. She kept praying about it and finally decided that it was, indeed, the will of God for her to marry this man. Yet, she still did not feel affectionate love for him. The more she waited on God, the more sure she was that she was to marry him, that he was the man God had for her as a life's companion.

She obeyed the Lord and agreed on a wedding date. As she started down that wedding aisle, she still was not feeling any physical love for the groom, but she was absolutely sure she was doing the right thing. When she said, "I do," and was swept into his arms, she was overwhelmed with a great surge of love for her husband that never faded until their dying day. Theirs was a romance and a love that was evident to all who knew them.

Now I would certainly not advise young people to wait until their wedding day to be sure they were in love. But it certainly worked in their case because they loved the Lord even more than they loved each other, and they knew they were in the will of God.

You can learn to love. Wait on God. Know His will. Be obedient. And He will lead you to the right mate and will bless and enhance your romance.

Just as we can learn to love the Lord more and more by spending much time with Him (in His Word, in prayer, in service), even so we can learn to love as we should in our relationships with others. Husbands and wives need to realize this. And any married couple who has had trouble with their marriage could learn to love again if they would give God a chance to help them and would be unselfish in their determination to make it work once more.

True love deepens as the days go by. Married people truly in love will find that the problems, heartaches, and burdens of having children, finding jobs, buying (or doing without) furniture, cars and other things will only make their love richer and fuller.

"Many waters cannot quench love, neither can the floods drown it" (Song of Sol. 8:7).

Questions

1. Why was Isaac able to love Rebekah with no problem?

2. What are some ways that we can learn to love?

55. Enjoy Your Marriage

Young couples get married with stars in their eyes and dreams of eternal happiness floating through their minds. They picture marriage as one glorious, perennial honeymoon! From television, songs, and novels, they anticipate a life of blisses and kisses. Then comes reality!

Married life like single life has its troubles, tests, and tribulations. Sicknesses come. Difficulties arise. Conflicts develop. Babies arrive. Often there is not enough money. Dispositions sour. Personalities clash. Weaklings rush to the divorce courts. The honey slowly drips out of the honeymoon!

Yet God says, "Rejoice with the wife of thy youth" (Prov. 5:18). He expects us to enjoy marriage. That's where true love comes in. Her love then will satisfy the husband at all times (Prov. 5:19), and he will be ravished with her charm and feminine loveliness. After God speaks of this, He proceeds to ask, "And why wilt thou, my son, be ravished with a strange woman, and embrace the bosom of a stranger?"

God always wants a man to "live joyfully with the wife" that he has chosen to love "all the days of the life . . . for that is thy portion in this life" (Eccles. 9:9). True love can overcome the sicknesses, sorrows, and situations that often strain a marriage. This will not be too difficult if God is their portion, a daily guide, and companion.

There are hundreds of happy Christian marriages across America, but watching TV and reading the world's periodicals make everything look bleak and hopeless.

The Song of Solomon does two things. It pictures the wonderful spiritual relationship between Christ and His church, and it is a wonderful story of the physical union of husband and wife—the intimacy of married love.

God tells wives to submit themselves unto their own husbands, "as unto the Lord" (Eph. 5). The husband is commanded to be the head of the wife, even as Christ is head of the church. The husband is commanded to love his wife even as Christ loved the church and gave Himself for it.

The husband is to love his wife so much that he would gladly be crucified for her. Men ought to love their wives as their own bodies. The man is to be "joined unto his wife, and they two shall be one flesh." Thus, the man is to "love his wife even as himself, and the wife see that she reverence her husband" (Eph. 5:31–33).

The Song of Solomon pictures the exquisite delight and rapture which married lovers feel for one another. So many times young people today are led to believe that their parents never make love, that there is no romance and joy in their marriage.

People who love one another as husband and wife and who keep the fire of love burning probably have more fun and excitement in their courting, embracing, and lovemaking than most people ever imagine. It gets sweeter as the years go by; true love ripens, deepens, and increases as the years go by. That's why some old people when they lose a wife or husband in death seem almost to wither away.

In the Song of Solomon when you read "I AM the rose of Sharon, and the lily of the valleys," you are reading about Christ, the heavenly Bridegroom. This is also true in "he is altogether lovely" (5:16). "Love is strong as death" (8:6) and "many waters cannot quench love" (8:7) refer to the love of Christ, but yet holds within it a picture of the kind of married love that God inspires.

When we read the sacred and intimate love scenes in which the bride and the bridegroom love, kiss, caress, and embrace one another, then we are glimpsing into the wonderful and personal delights of a husband and wife who are learning the unsearchable pleasure of physical union. "My beloved is mine, and I am his" (Song of Sol. 2:16). "Behold, thou art fair, my love," the bridegroom says (4:1). "Thou hast ravished my heart" (4:9).

"I sleep, but my heart waketh," cries the bride (5:2). She thinks of her lover-husband even when she sleeps. Her dreams are filled with these luscious thoughts of love. When she for awhile is separated from him, she becomes "sick of love" (5:8); in other words she is lovesick. Often when married lovers have to be apart for awhile, their hearts at times literally ache for the other!

The Song of Solomon assures us that God meant for married love to be enjoyed!

Question

1. How does Ephesians 5 relate to the Song of Solomon?

2. How much is a man supposed to love his wife?

3. How is the wife to think of her husband?

56. "How Shall I Love Thee?"

Every couple wants a happy love life and marriage. The secret of it is found in Ephesians 5. Here we are told that the wife is to be in sweet submission unto her husband and the husband is to love his wife as himself. If you learn these principles while you are young, you can save yourself grief when you come to your own marriage.

"Neither was the man created for the woman, but the woman for the man" (1 Cor. 11:9). God made Eve to help, assist, love, and care for Adam. The greatest career a woman can have is to be the devoted wife of a good man and the mother of happy, successful children, all of them living to glorify God. We cannot have the man without the woman, or the woman without the man. God distinguishes the authority of the man and the glory of the woman.

The wife is commanded to submit herself unto her husband "as unto the Lord" (Eph. 5:22). In other words her sweet submission to her husband will be as unto the Lord because she believes the Lord knows best and has a good reason for making man the head of the home. And the husband is the head of the wife even as Christ is head of the church. A body with two heads would indeed be a freak. With both husband and wife trying to "rule the roost," this two-headed monster always creates trouble! "Let the wives be (subject) to their own husbands in everything" (Eph. 5:24).

"How shall I love thee?" Many a man is short on his end of the team. For he is commanded, "Husbands, love your wives, even as Christ also loved the church, and gave himself for it" (Eph. 5:25). A husband is commanded to love his wife like Christ loved the church: fervently, kindly, graciously, patiently, tenderly, sacrificially! Two people who live according to these Biblical rules can never break up their home.

When married, two become "one flesh." Two are as if the two were one. Each belongs to the other. The man should love his wife as his own body (Eph 5:28). As he loves his wife so he loves himself. After all, she is his, he chose her. He can't abuse her or be unkind to her. This is why divorce is such a wretched, wrenching, crushing thing. It is like the breaking of the bones and the rending of the flesh. God never intended for marriages to break up. Never plan on it; don't even think about it!

The happy, devoted Christian couple can be hilariously content and joyful in their marriage even after many years. "This is a great mystery," but it is like the love of Christ for His church. It will be as mysterious to the world when they look on a happy, successful marriage as it is when they view the amazing grace and love of Christ for His people, the church.

So the man should love his wife as much as he loves (values and thinks of) himself, and the wife is to "reverence her husband!" The woman who reverences her husband will sweetly submit to his leadership and not want to displease him (Eph. 5:32–33).

Christians are prone to blame their meanness and rebellion on the Devil, who is very real and hates happy, pure Christians and successful marriages, but the Devil cannot *make* you do wrong if you determine not to! (1 Pet. 5:8).

"Resist the devil, and he will flee from you" (James 4:7). "Neither give place to the devil" (Eph. 4:27). Don't give Satan a landing strip in your marriage. Stand steadfast. "Make no provision for the flesh." Satan will tempt couples both before and after marriage to take forbidden fruit and play loose morally. But God says, "Fornication, and all uncleanness, or covetousness, let it not be once named among you" (Eph. 5:3). Don't name it, don't talk about it, don't even consider it!

Don't dwell on such matters. Don't let the soap operas and worldly movies and songs tempt you. God says, "I would have you wise unto that which is good, and simple concerning evil" (Rom. 16:19).

Memorize 1 Corinthians 10:13, which states that God is faithful to see you through any temptation and make a way of escape always. He knows what you are able to bear. He will give the victory "through Christ which strengtheneth me" (Phil. 4:13).

Questions

1. In Ephesians 5 how does God picture the husband and wife?

2. How is the wife to submit to her husband?

3. How does Eph. 5:25 reveal that a husband is never to be a cruel dictator in the home?

57. Maintaining a Happy Home

The happiest homes are those devoted to Christ where each member of the family is obedient to God's Word. Titus 2:2–9 gives good counsel on maintaining a happy home.

The older men (fathers and grandfathers) are to be sober, grave (serious about serious things), temperate (controlled appetites), sound in faith (Biblically correct), sound in charity (love) and patience also. They are to be the stalwart pillars of the home, showing love and patience to the weak and younger members.

The mothers, grandmothers, older aunts, are to be godly in behavior, "teachers of good things" "not false accusers" as gossipers and busybodies. "Not given to wine" or anything else that would be a bad example.

The younger women should learn what is good from the older women in the family. Thus they will be sober (temperate and thoughtful) and will love their husbands and their children. Loving their children will make them good mothers, for they will seek always those things that are best for their children and will train them diligently. They are to be discreet (showing good conduct), chaste (modest and decent), keepers at home (meaning that they will put the home first, not neglecting home duties), good, obedient to their own husbands (not rebellious and belligerent), "that the word of God be not blasphemed."

Young men are to be sober minded, not foolish, in all things showing a "pattern of good works." Somebody is deciding today what they will do with their lives by the "pattern" they see in your life and mine.

Parents will set a good example by being true to their own husband or wife, remembering that "marriage is honourable in all, and the (marriage) bed undefiled" (Heb. 13:4). They will prove by their own happiness together that married adults know a warm joy in their love lives far superior to anything a lost, wicked, and adulterous world could ever imagine.

Children, thus, will grow up "in the nurture and admonition of the Lord" (Eph. 6:4). Begin now, as a young person, to prepare for that successful marriage you will one day enjoy.

Questions

1. *How are older people in the home to help the younger?*

2. *Name some qualities God expects from young mothers.*

58. Adultery and Divorce

Jesus talked about divorce, not because He approved of it, but because the breaking up of marriages is an ugly fact of life. It is assumed that once a marriage takes place, sexual union will follow. This is God's plan—one man with one woman! "What God hath joined together, let not man put asunder." This is why years ago if a young man "violated" a young lady—in other words had sexual union with her—the honorable thing for him to do was to marry the girl. This kept a young man thinking seriously, for, if he was not ready to marry the girl, he had better behave himself; otherwise, her dad might come with a shotgun and a preacher!

After marrying the girl, the husband is expected by God to remain true to her "until death do them part." The only definite clear-cut reason for divorce allowed by God is adultery. In other words, if one's mate ran off with and lived with another person intimately, a divorce would be permitted or tolerated.

"Thou shalt not commit adultery," Jesus quoted from the ten commandments; then He said that some men commited adultery in their hearts (Matt. 5:27–28) by looking on and lusting after another woman. The looking leads to longing, and the longing to lusting, which leads to disaster! Jesus said that it would be better to pluck out an offensive eye rather than look and lust that leads to ruin in this life and Hell in the next life.

Jesus said that divorce was permitted under the law of Moses for "the hardness of your hearts" (Matt. 19:8) but in the beginning this was never God's plan nor intention for man. In the New Testament, Jesus says, "That whosoever shall put away his wife, saving for the cause of fornication, causeth her to commit adultery: and whosoever shall marry her that is divorced committeth adultery" (Matt. 5:32).

Jesus further explained, "Whosoever shall put away his wife, except it be for fornication, and shall marry another, committeth adultery: and whoso marrieth her which is put away doth commit adultery" (Matt. 19:9). He says that a man is not to divorce his wife (or vice versa) unless she has been involved in fornication (adultery) with another, and the man divorcing his wife and marrying again is himself committing adultery. He also says that the man who marries the woman who has been divorced commits adultery.

Jesus does not say that a man *has* to divorce his wife even if she *is* guilty of fornication. And the Bible does not teach that a woman *has* to divorce her husband because he has been unfaithful. They are permitted to, but not commanded to. Divorce is still not the answer. Most people could work it out if they would really try, and let God help them. And especially, where children are involved, couples should move heaven and earth to work it out!

Where the man and wife are both Christians, there is no reason they could not before God repent, renew their vows, seek God's face earnestly, and save their marriage for the glory of God and the good of their family. Jesus taught that it is "from within, out of the heart of men," that adulteries and fornications come as well as murders, thefts, blasphemies, etc. (Mark 7:21).

People today get divorces on the grounds of mental cruelty, incompatibility, even trivial things like irritability or laziness. Why is this wrong? This shows sin in the heart, blossoming as selfishness, which is responsible for most divorces. Lust and ignorance could be cured by unselfishness. Determine now that you will not marry until you have surrendered the matter to God and are sure that He is leading in this important event in your life.

Questions

1. *Give the one reason Christ would permit a divorce.*

2. *Where did Jesus say adulteries come from?*

59. Consequences of an Affair

Man always wants to tone down the severity of his sin. So today adultery and fornication are often referred to as "an affair." These "affairs" in immorality always bring heartache, problems, disappointment, and frequently total ruin.

The Thirsty Woman

Jesus encountered the Samaritan woman at the well. The woman He met at Jacob's well had quite a past. She had lived with five "husbands." Whether she was legally married to all five we do not know. But she had lived with five men and now was living with a sixth man to whom she was not married. She was a "common law" wife.

Until recently, in America it was almost unheard of for a man and woman to live together without benefit of a marriage ceremony. Anyone who did such a thing was considered a common harlot or a cheap, morally degenerate person at best. It is still considered morally wrong by most people, frowned on by Bible believing churches, and there are still laws against such adultery in many places. Though America has sunk morally low in recent years, however, sin is still sin! God has not changed His mind about adultery.

The woman at the well truly had "no husband" even though she lived with a man (John 4:17, 18). Was this poor woman happy? Not at all!

She had some religious background but never knew the way of salvation. She probably was attractive, or had been, for that many men to be interested in her. (Sometimes being attractive can be the undoing of a girl—it brings temptations she never would have had otherwise.) She was not an uneducated person. She spoke well, and she knew about the promised Messiah. She was energetic, for after she discovered who Jesus really was she ran back to the city to tell her men friends that she had been saved. She became a soulwinner at once. This woman never found what she was looking for until she found Jesus. Her "affairs" were over.

We may be sure that the woman at the well either married the man she lived with or that he soon "had his walking papers." The good news here is that no matter how dark and bleak the past may have been, the Lord can transform even a woman like this.

Caught Red-Handed

The religious hypocrites of that day brought to Jesus a woman who had been caught in the act of adultery. It is significant that they did not bring the *man*. Too often the woman has had to take the blame in such matters, but God holds the man just as responsible. These religious hypocrites wanted the woman to be stoned to death, which was the penalty under the Mosiac law. But Jesus forgave her and told her to "go, and sin no more" (John 8:11).

Such sin is always wrong. You can be sure that there were always scars that remained in the lives of both the woman at the well and the woman taken in adultery. But God can forgive and cleanse, if we'll truly repent and trust in Him to do so. None of us are without sin (of one kind or another), so we should look with kindness, tenderness, and pity upon those who have fallen. And, if one reads these lines who has fallen into such sin, remember that "though your sins be as scarlet, they shall be as white as snow" (Isa. 1:18), if you truly repent (turn from your sin) and receive His wonderful grace and forgiveness.

The Alabaster Box

Another New Testament instance of divine forgiveness for such sin is found in Luke 7. This woman "which was a sinner" is found weeping, washing the feet of Jesus with her tears, and wiping them with the long hair of her head. Finally, she anointed His feet with precious ointment. Here is a beautiful picture of true repentance: She came to Jesus, wept true tears of repentance, served Jesus, and bestowed a lavish gift upon Him.

But the scars remain. You can pull nails out of a post, but the gashes and holes are still there. It is far better never to fall into sin, for scars will always be there to mark the "affair."

Questions

1. Why do men today want to call the terrible sin of adultery simply "an affair"?

2. What was her great concern after the woman at the well was converted?

3. What did Jesus tell the woman taken in adultery?

60. Jealousy—the Death of Romance

The Bible speaks of the spirit of jealousy coming upon a man and the results that follow (Num. 5:14). The "spirit of jealousy" can come on a man or a woman when there is no real cause for jealousy. "Jealousy is the rage of a man" (Prov. 6:34). People sometimes become jealous for no reason.

Allowing yourself to be physically involved with a boyfriend or girlfriend can make that person feel that he or she "owns" you. Then when you see your friend with another, it causes jealousy.

Husbands and wives who love each other and are absolutely faithful to their own mates should have little or no cause to be jealous. It is wise to be very careful never to give our loved ones cause for jealousy.

Solomon said "Jealousy is cruel as the grave" (Song of Sol. 8:6). He ought to know, for he probably observed much of it among his many wives.

Married people should be perfectly honest with their mates, and young people should be honest with their friends. "She (a wife) that maketh ashamed is as rottenness in his bones"

(Prov. 12:4). We should do nothing to make those we love, or care about be ashamed of our behavior.

King Saul started out as a great king, but he let jealousy ruin him. He heard the young women shouting the praises of young David returning as victor of the battle, "Saul hath slain his thousands, and David his ten thousands" (1 Sam. 18:7). Saul was smitten with the green-eyed monster of jealousy and from then on he attempted to slay David, his finest warrior and the best friend of his son Jonathan.

Many atrocious crimes are committed because of jealousy. Young people who keep themselves sexually pure until they are married will be able to avoid much of the grief that jealousy brings.

Questions

1. *Why could Solomon know so much about jealousy?*

2. *How does physical affection on the part of single young people bring about waves of jealousy?*

SEX, PURITY, AND THE JUDGMENT OF GOD

61. Stay Sound to Stay Safe

It does matter what we believe. Anything that is not Scripturally sound is false doctrine. God wants us to be sound in the faith. "The time will come when they will not endure sound doctrine" (2 Tim. 4:3). Only by "sound doctrine" can we exhort and convince the gainsayers (Titus 1:9–10). We are to speak "the things which become sound doctrine" (Titus 2:1). We are to "hold fast the form of sound words" (2 Tim. 1:13).

What does this have to do with sex and purity? God warns that in these last days there will be many who are "having a form of godliness, but denying the power thereof: from such turn away. For of this sort are they which creep into houses, and lead captive silly women laden with sins, led away with divers lusts" (2 Tim. 3:5). Those who are not Biblically sound but merely have "a form of godliness" are the most likely to be led off into sin by silly women who are laden with sins. Remember this when you hear of a theological student or a compromising preacher going into immorality. God teaches that sound doctrine and sound living go hand in hand.

When the giant falls, there is a reason. I've seen a great tree in the forest fall while many smaller trees stayed upright. Why? Upon close investigation we found that the big tree was really rotten on the inside! If one has rotten doctrine, he may soon fall into rotten sin. If, on the other hand, an apparently sound Christian begins to dabble in sin, he will soon be toning down the strength and soundness of his doctrine.

God commands preachers to "preach the word" (2 Tim. 4). Many do not do so. They preach nice things, some of which they find in the Bible. They may even preach the gospel. But if they are truly sound in the faith, they will preach the whole counsel of God. They will warn against sin. They will be faithful to proclaim the Bible and expose false doctrine to keep their people out of trouble. The man is not your friend who knows that the bridge is out down the road but lets you drive on with a cheery smile to your doom.

These compromising, professional preachers "turn away their ears from the truth, and shall be turned unto fables." It is no wonder that this kind of spiritual leader is "drawn away of his own lust, and enticed" (James 1:14). Those who have fables in their doctrine may well have folly in their moral lives.

Jude faithfully warns us that these are men, "crept in unawares," who were "ordained to this condemnation," are "ungodly men, turning the grace of our God into lasciviousness (meaning lewd, lustful), and denying the only Lord God, and our Lord Jesus Christ." So the Bible indicates that lewd, lustful living often goes with loose, compromising preaching! We need to stay sound in doctrine to stay safe in morals.

We see that evil doctrine and evil, impure acts go hand in hand as a wicked prophetess (woman preacher) in the church at Thyatira who, while calling herself a prophetess (pretending to be a servant of the Lord), was really teaching her listeners "to commit fornication, and to eat things sacrificed to idols" (Rev. 2:20).

John warns that we should "try the spirits whether they are of God" (1 John 4:1), "because many false prophets are gone out into the world." This is important to know because so many people today think if one is a religious leader, he must be of God.

Jesus warned, "Beware of false prophets, which come to you in sheep's clothing, but inwardly they are ravening wolves" (Matt. 7:15).

Questions

1. What does God mean by sound doctrine?

2. If one is unsound or weak in Bible knowledge what may happen?

3. What did Jesus say about false prophets and sheep's clothing?

62. Should the Priest Get Married?

The Spirit of God warns us about temptations in the last days before the return of Christ. Some will "depart from the faith, giving heed to seducing spirits and doctrines of devils; Speaking lies in hypocrisy; having their conscience seared with a hot iron.

"Forbidding to marry, and commanding to abstain from meats, which God hath created to be received with thanksgiving of them which believe and know the truth" (1 Tim. 4). There are certain religions who have "priests," who are "forbidden to marry." The leaders of the New Testament churches are not called priests but pastors, sometimes called elders or bishops.

Priests were in the Old Testament under the Mosiac law. They were Jews. The only priests in the New Testament are believers—those who are true Christians. The book of Hebrews speaks of the priesthood of the believers.

So unlike the Jewish believer under the Mosiac law, we do not have a priest to go into God's presence for us, but every believer has the wonderful privilege of going right into the throne room of heaven by faith in Christ. (John 14:6; Heb. 10:19–22). Jesus Christ is our High Priest. (Heb. 4:14–16).

Nowhere in the Bible are we told that the priest should never marry; it was the "seducing spirits and doctrines of devils" that gave such a command that the priest was forbidden to marry (1 Tim. 4:1–3). It is an unnatural and, for many, an unholy command. This is one reason why so many priests have been charged with homosexual vice, even to the seducing of young boys under their charge.

God speaks of those who have broken the laws of God, such as "them that defile themselves with mankind" (1 Tim. 1:10), in other words those who practice homosexuality. When many men who have a natural longing to be married are "forbidden to marry," they thus often are driven into unnatural perversion.

If you are saved, then you are a priest unto God (Rev. 1:6), and God certainly does not forbid you to marry. But God does give some definite counsel to the young believer. We are to intreat the elder Christian man as a father, and the younger men as brothers (1 Tim. 5). We are to look upon the older women as we would our mothers and the younger girls as sisters "with all purity." Treat women and girls as you would want others to treat your mother and sisters. This will keep many a young man straight. We are to think about men and boys as we would our own Dad and brothers.

Questions

1. Where does the teaching that a priest should not marry nor eat certain meats come from?

2. Where in the Bible are men called priests and what kind of priests were they?

3. In the New Testament who is called a priest?

63. Eunuchs in the Bible

Eunuchs in old times were "bed keepers" who took care of the private rooms of royal and prominent people. They were private maids (if a man can be called a maid), and because of jealousy on the part of royal despots, they were frequently (but not always) deprived of their manhood—in other words, rendered sexless by surgery, or robbed of their virility. This was especially true if they were in charge of a harem. These eunuchs would never marry nor have families; they would devote their whole life to serving the king.

Eunuchs with ability, who proved faithful and loyal to their masters, were given responsibility accordingly in the kingdom. Such were the young and very wise eunuchs mentioned in the book of Daniel. In fact, Daniel, a eunuch, helped guide the entire kingdom of Babylon and the Medes and the Persian empire.

The Ethiopian eunuch in Acts 8 was a man of great authority who had the charge of all the treasury of the Queen of Ethiopia. He was the financial business head who faithfully served the Queen in business matters. Jesus taught that some eunuchs were born that way, while others (like many in the Old Testament) had been made eunuchs by men. Jesus does not condemn eunuchs at all. He said that there are some eunuchs who have purposely made themselves so "for the kingdom of heaven's sake" (Matt. 19:12). In other words, there are some men who love the Lord so much and who feel that they can do without the warmth of married love in order to devote themselves completely to serving the Lord. I have known some missionaries like this. I have also known some people working in churches who I believe are as pure as fresh fallen snow and are so taken up with the things of God that sexual desire does not concern them.

Questions

1. What did the Ethiopian in Acts 8 and the wise men of Daniel's time have in common?

2. Why did Jesus say some men have "made themselves eunuchs"?

64. Spiritual Adultery

We have learned that God hates the sin of adultery and fornication. But now we find there is another kind of adultery, "Ye adulterers and adulteresses, know ye not that the friendship of the world is enmity with God? whosoever therefore will be a friend of the world is the enemy of God" (James 4:4). God says if we are friends of this world and run with the world and are devoted to this world system, we are guilty of spiritual adultery and are therefore "the enemies of God!"

"Love not the world, neither the things that are in the world. If any man love the world, the love of the Father is not in him" (1 John 2:15). So while we are *in* the world, we are not to be *of* the world. Our citizenship is in heaven; we belong to a far better world.

"For all that is in the world, the lust of the flesh, and the lust of the eyes, and the pride of life, is not of the Father, but is of the world. And the world passeth away, and the lust thereof: but he that doeth the will of God abideth for ever" (1 John 2:16–17). It is easy to see here that the things that captivate us and appeal to our fleshly nature so that we lust after these things are displeasing to God. What appeals to the flesh? Money, for one thing. But we have to have money to live. Yes, but God says, "the **love** of money is the root of all evil"

(1 Tim. 6:10). We are not to **love** the world or worldly things. It is not wrong to enjoy the beautiful world of nature that God has made, but we are not to love these legitimate things so much that it blinds us to the love of Christ or consumes our thinking and energies so that we do not put Him first.

It is not wrong to enjoy nice clothes, cars, or houses. But as Christians we are to be careful that we are not so taken up with these things and delighted in them that we are guilty of spiritual adultery because these things can become an idol to us and mean more to us than God!

God mentions "the lust of the flesh," and the "lust of the eyes." What do our eyes constantly behold? How much do we see television? Are we tempted to patronize the movie theater? Do we read questionable books or let our eyes feast upon lewd magazines?

"The pride of life" can be a snare and also lead one into spiritual adultery. Remember, pride goes before a fall. Young people are not the only ones who fall. Often mature Christians, even preachers and Christian workers, are smitten with pride. Their "pride of life" in things that are religious, righteous, nice, and clean, can become a temptation to spiritual pride. Success in Christian work can trip us.

Let's be careful, God is saying, that we not so love, admire, and covet the goods, friends, money, fame, or applause of this world that we are tricked into spiritual adultery. This whole world system is against God.

A great world-famous, false religion that has dominated and controlled the lives of multiplied millions of people and still does, will be destroyed during the Great Tribulation (Rev. 17:1–7). God calls this religious system "the great whore" (harlot). Kings and leaders of nations have been intoxicated with the wine of her fornication. So false religion is spiritual adultery and fornication!

Spiritual adultery abounds on every hand today as God prepares the world for the judgment that the world has brought upon itself.

Stay true to God and the Bible. Live a separated life, and you'll not be guilty of spiritual adultery.

Questions

1. *We are called "enemies of God" when we are guilty of spiritual adultery. What does this mean?*

2. *Why is it dangerous to love this world?*

65. Filthy Dreamers

Jude urges us to "contend for the faith" because there will be certain men creeping into the religious world who will turn "the grace of God into lasciviousness (lewd and lustful living)." He calls them filthy dreamers who defile the flesh; he describes the hearts of people in general in the last days before the return of Christ.

Sodom and Gomorrha were the two cities that were blasted into oblivion (Gen. 19) because of their vile sins of homosexual vice. They were given over to fornication and went after "strange flesh." Today people are constantly talking about fornication (in books, magazines, jokes, music, TV, movies, advertising, conversation), and sodomy is glorified as the "gay" movement.

Jude reminds us that the sodomites going after strange (or prohibited) flesh are following the "example" of the Genesis outbreak who suffered "the vengeance of eternal fire." As "brute beasts" they "corrupt themselves."

Of course all sex sinners are not perverted sodomites. Peter describes the average lost person who follows "the will of the Gentiles," walking "in lasciviousness, lusts, excess of wine, revellings (dancing, etc.), banquetings (overindulgence), and abominable idolatries" (1 Pet. 4:3). They fill the movie theaters, night clubs, bars, brothels, gambling dens, and hotel ballrooms of the world.

"Having eyes full of adultery," God says about those filthy dreamers who think about sex all the time. They dwell upon lust so much that they "dream" of adultery day and night. They are constantly looking at and dwelling upon evil and are continually looking over the situation for their next conquest in adultery. This is the most popular theme of Hollywood movies today.

"Testimony has been wrung from millions of people in every age and in every land that they have made their lives a horror, deliberately indulging a passion which destroyed them, body, soul, and spirit. To try to make headway against the force of such evidence is like trying to climb up the Niagara Falls. "Resist the siren voice that calls you to your doom!" are the words of an old divine.

"They think it strange that ye run not with them to the same excess of riot, speaking evil of you" (1 Pet. 4:4). Have you ever been criticized, vilified, or hounded because you would not go to the prom, the rock concert, or the drive-in theater? Have you ever been considered "square" because you don't have rock records or don't read dirty books? Do your relatives think you're too narrow because you have standards and dare to be a consecrated and separated Christian?

Well, join the club! Real Christians have always had to take persecution, misunderstanding, and ostracism. But remember what the payoff will be one day when you stand before God. It does pay to serve Jesus!

Learn to hate evil, "hating even the garment spotted by the flesh" (Jude 23). Ask God to empower you to "abhor that which is evil" (Rom. 12:9). "Put on the whole armour of God" (Eph. 6). Hate dirty language, dirty music, dirty films and books. "Cleave to that which is good." Hate the things that God hates and love the things that God loves. He is able to keep us from falling and to present us faultless before Him one day in heaven.

Questions

1. *What cities went after "strange flesh" as a warning to us today?*

2. *What does "strange flesh" mean?*

The Final Judgment
66. of the Sexually Impure

We will each give account of ourselves when we "tell it to the Judge"! That judge is the Judge of the universe. If this life were all, it would still pay to be pure in heart and action. But this life is not all, and we must one day face the judgment bar of God.

After many frightening plagues of war and judgment during the Great Tribulation, we read, "Neither repented they of their murders, nor of their sorceries, nor of their fornication, nor of their thefts" (Rev. 9:21).

God says that the abominable and the whoremongers are cast into the lake of fire and brimstone right along with the murderers, sorcerers, idolaters, all liars, and the "fearful and unbelieving" (Rev. 21:8). Those who are so "fearful" of what people say that they pay no attention to what God says, and the "unbelieving"—those who refuse to believe God, make their own beds in hell.

Those "without" are shut out from God's presence and from God's heaven through all eternity. The morally impure (fornicators, adulterers, perverts) are described with one word, "whoremongers," and they are put in the class of "dogs" (moral tramps—not four-legged animals), sorcerers (those who delve into drugs, witchcraft, etc.), murderers, idolaters, etc. This is the final judgment of the sexually impure. Has their brief lifetime fling in lust and evil been worth it? No, not in the light of eternity!

So God's hatred for sin is evident throughout the Bible, even as His love for sinners is also revealed. For those not saved, He says, "Come. And let him that is athirst come. And whosoever will, let him take the water of life freely" (Rev. 22:17). Christ died for sinners. Admit you are a sinner, repent (turn from your sin to the Savior), and believe on Him—(trust Him, receive Him, rely upon Him) to save you. It's as simple as that!

After you are saved, read and study the Bible daily. Pray about everything. Cultivate the presence of God. Die to yourself daily (ask God at the beginning of each day to take control of your life for that day). Be filled with the Spirit. Attend a Bible-believing, evangelistic church.

If possible, attend a good Christian school with high moral standards. Make plans to attend a truly spiritual Christian college.

Make friends of God's children. Read good books. Serve the Lord with gladness.

A Beka Book Publications, a division of Pensacola Christian College, is a Christian textbook ministry designed to meet the need for Christian textbooks and teaching aids. The purpose of this publications ministry is to help Christian schools reach children and young people for the Lord and train them in the Christian way of life.

If we can be of further help to your ministry, please write *A Beka Book Publications,* Box 18000, Pensacola, Florida 32523-9160.